Get Connected ...

Explore ...

Succeed!

Open Road Companion Website

www.longmanesl.ca/gaetz.cw

Improve your English skills:

- Interactive activities to practise the four skills: reading, writing, speaking, and listening
- Vocabulary review exercises for each chapter
- Variety of exercise types: fill-in-the-blank, matching, multiple-choice
- Model essays, summaries, and oral reports
- Links to websites related to the content of each chapter

To access the Companion Website

Step 1 Go to **www.longmanesl.ca/gaetz.cw**

Step 2 Choose **Open Road**.

Step 3 When asked, enter the following username and password:

Username

Password

This textbook **cannot be returned** if the label is removed.

PEEL OFF HERE

Step 4 Follow the instructions on the screen.

Note to Teachers

To obtain a username and password that will allow you to access the Teacher Section of the Companion Website, please contact your Pearson Longman ESL consultant.

Technical Support: tech@erpi.com

10810W

English Skills

Open Road

Second Edition

English Skills

Open Road

Second Edition

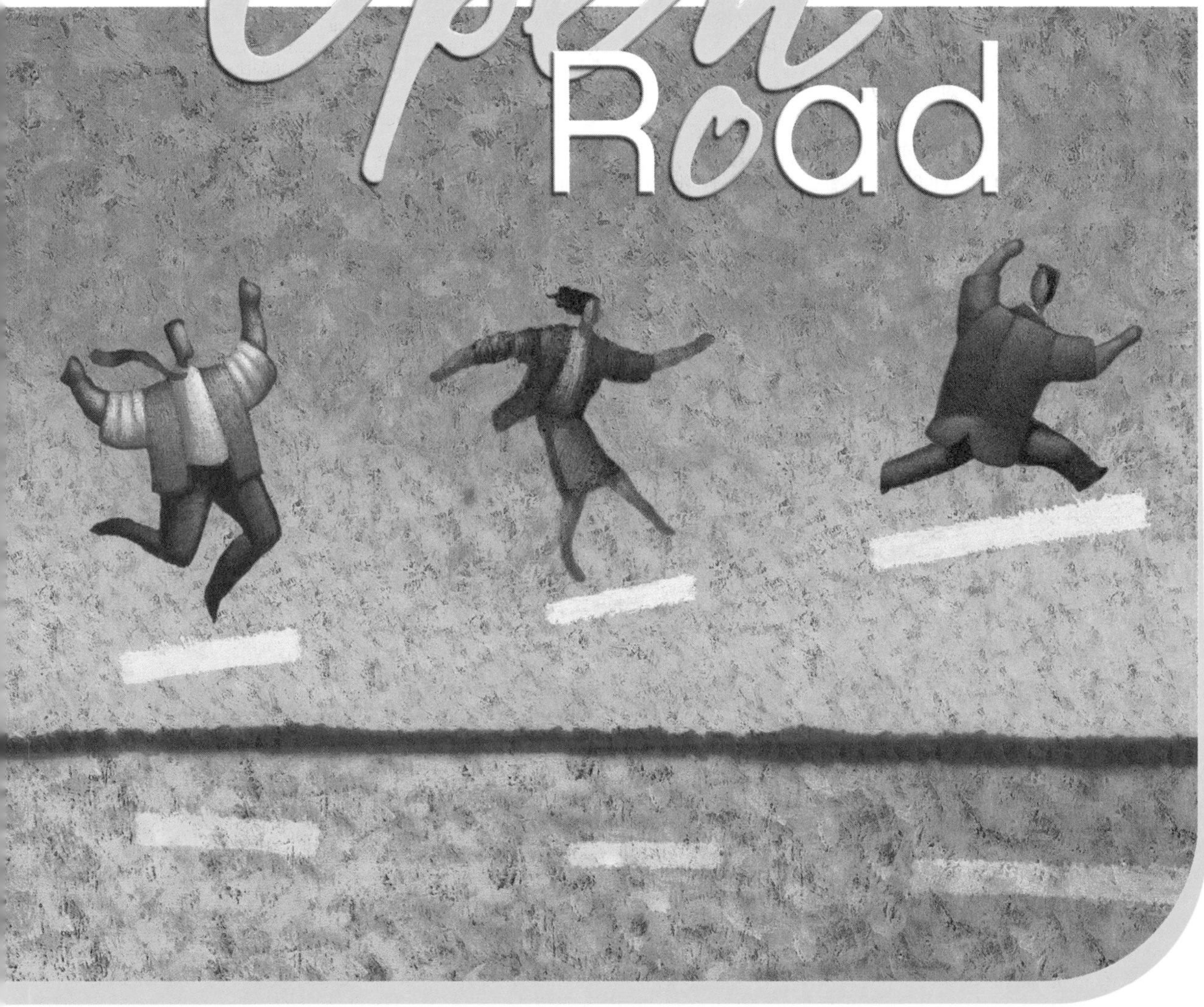

Lynne Gaetz
Collège Lionel-Groulx

COMPANION WEBSITE BY
BRENT DAVIS REID
Collège de Bois-de-Boulogne

DISTRIBUTED IN CANADA BY ERPI
5757, RUE CYPIHOT, SAINT-LAURENT (QUÉBEC) H4S 1R3
TELEPHONE: (514) 334-2690 ext. 232 FAX: (514) 334-0448
infoesl@erpi.com www.longmanesl.ca

ACKNOWLEDGEMENTS

I would like to express sincere thanks to:

- Lucie Turcotte for her patience and insights while editing this book
- Sharnee Chait and My-Trang Nguyen for their invaluable editing
- Dominique Gagnon and the team at Dessine-moi un mouton
- Brent Davis Reed for his wonderful work on the companion website
- Dorothy Nixon, Luna Tarlo, Line Bechard and Naomi Louder for their important contributions.
- Liz Gagnon for her great work on the video and audio transcripts
- My students and colleagues at College Lionel-Groulx
- My colleagues throughout the province who kindly provided feedback:

Margaret Chell (Collège Ahuntsic)
Jany Couture (Cégep Marie-Victorin)
Michel Lacroix (Collège Gérald-Godin)
Sharon Ney-Durocher (Cégep de Jonquière)

Finally, I extend special thanks to my husband and children.

Managing Editor
Sharnee Chait

Editor
Lucie Turcotte

Copy Editor
My-Trang Nguyen

Proofreader
Katya Epstein

Art Director
Hélène Cousineau

Book design
Dessine-moi un mouton
Pige Communication

Cover and page layout
Dessine-moi un mouton

  Published and distributed by

ÉDITIONS DU RENOUVEAU PÉDAGOGIQUE INC.

Registration of copyright: Bibliothèque et Archives nationales du Québec, 2007
Registration of copyright : Library and Archives Canada 2007
Printed in Canada

ISBN 978-2-7613-1903-4

456789 II 09
10810 ABCD OF-10

CREDITS

The following authors, publishers, and photographers have generously given permission to reprint copyright material.

Chapter 1 p. 1-12 Tahitian Landscape with a Mountain (1893) by Paul Gauguin (1848-1903; French). Oil on canvas, Minneapolis Institute of Art, Minneapolis, Minnesota. © SuperStock, Inc. p. 3 "How Travel Has Changed My Life" by Arthur Frommer reprinted from Arthur Frommer's Budget Travel Online (http://www.frommers.com/). p. 4 Photograph of a Chinese marketplace © Jupiterimages. p. 6 Audio text "Travel Stories from Syria" © Canadian Broadcasting Corporation. p. 7 "The Longest Ride" by Rob Penn © Rob Penn. Reprinted by permission of the author. p. 8 Photograph of bicycle © Rubén Hidalgo / iStockphoto.

Chapter 2 p. 13-24 Photograph © kutay tanir / iStockphoto. p. 14 "My Dates with a Rock Star" by Chloe Cantrell reprinted by permission of Naomi Louder; photograph of guitar © Neil Sullivan / iStockphoto. p. 17 Video Segment "The Hero Among Us" © Canadian Broadcasting Corporation. p. 18 "Che Today" by Larry Rohter originally published under the title "Che Today? More Easy Rider than Revolutionary" in *The New York Times*, April 26, 2005. Copyright © 2005 by The New York Times Co. Reprinted with permission. p. 19 Photograph of Che Guevara © Topham Picturepoint / Topfoto / PONOPRESSE. p. 21 "Che Guevara: The Killing Machine" by Alvaro Vargas Llosa originally published under the title "The Killing Machine: Che Guevara, from Communist Firebrand to Capitalist Brand," July 11, 2005. Reprinted from http://www.independent.org/newsroom by permission of the author. p. 23 Audio text "Sports Heroes" © National Public Radio; photograph of basketball player © Dean Fox / SuperStock.

Chapter 3 p. 25-39 Photograph of archer from Photothèque ERPI. p. 28 "Racism's Source" by Gwynne Dyer originally published under the title "Racism is Panicky Reaction to Change" in *The Montreal Gazette*, August 26, 2000. Reprinted by permission of the author; "New Orinics Party" by Graham Knuttel (b. 1954; Irish); New Apollo Gallery, Dublin. © New Apollo Gallery / SuperStock. p. 30 "P Is for Prejudice" by Allen Abel © 2001. Reprinted with permission of the author. p 35 Audio Text "Pakistan" © Canadian Broadcasting Corporation. p. 36 Photograph of wooden carved statues of Native Americans © Dean Fox / SuperStock; "Seeing Red over Myths" by Drew Hayden Taylor © 2001 Drew Hayden Taylor. Reprinted by permission of the author.

Chapter 4 p. 40-52 Photograph of Times Square © Ingram Publishing / SuperStock. p. 42 "Put GI Barbie in the Bargain Bin" by Dorothy Nixon reprinted by permission of the author. p. 43 Photograph of boy's toys © David Spindel / SuperStock; photograph of girl's toys © Michel Ponomareff / PONOPRESSE. p. 45 Audio text "The Age of Persuasion" © Canadian Broadcasting Corporation. p. 47 "The Night the Martians Attacked" by Lee Krystek © Lee Krystek / The Museum of Unnatural Mystery. Reprinted by permission of the author; "High angle view of a flying saucer" © Dale O'Dell / SuperStock. p. 50 Video segment "JFK: What's Fact, What's Not" © Canadian Broadcasting Corporation; photograph of J. F. Kennedy and his wife © Topham Picturepoint / Topfoto / PONOPRESSE.

Chapter 5 p. 53-66 Photograph of a camera © René Mansi / iStockphoto; photographs A, C, and D © Jupiterimages; photograph B, "Group of people playing mahjong on the street, Beijing, China" © Steve Vidler / SuperStock. p. 54 Video segment "Unreliable Evidence" © Canadian Broadcasting Corporation. p. 58 Excerpt from "The Memory Wars" by Elizabeth Loftus, reprinted from the March-April 2004 issue of *Science and Spirit* magazine (www.science-spirit.org). © Elizabeth Loftus. Reprinted with permission; "Portrait—After Van der Weyden, by Donald Martin (20th C.; American); airbrush on wood, private collection. © Donald C. Martin / SuperStock. p. 60 Audio text "Crime Scene Witness" © Canadian Broadcasting Corporation. p. 62 "My African Childhood" reprinted from *Me Talk Pretty One Day* by David Sedaris. Copyright © 2000 by David Sedaris. By permission of Little, Brown, and Co., Inc.

Chapter 6 p. 67-83 "Good and Evil" (detail) (1832) by André Jacques Victor Orsel (1795-1850; French), Musée des Beaux-Arts, Lyon, France. © Peter Willi / SuperStock. p. 69 "Resisting Authority" by Joseph Dimow first published in the January-February 2004 issue of *Jewish Currents* (http://www.Jewishcurrents.org/2004-jan-dimow.htm); photographs from the film Obedience © 1968 by Stanley Milgram, © Renewed 1993 by Alexandra Milgram, and distributed by Penn State, Media Sales. p. 74 Audio text "Human Behaviour Experiments" © Canadian Broadcasting Corporation. p. 75 "The Stanford Prison Experiment" by Kathleen O'Toole from the Stanford University News Service (www.stanford.edu/dept/news/index.html). Reprinted by permission of Kathleen O'Toole, Stanford News Service; "Zimbardo's Stanford Prison Experiment" photograph © Philip G. Zimbardo, Inc. p. 77 Video segment "The Power of the Situation" © Annenberg Media. p. 80 "Conscience" from *Numbers in the Dark* by Italo Calvino (pp. 18-19). English translation by Tim Parks. Published by Alfred A. Knopf Canada and Pantheon Books (a division of Random House) in the US. 1993.

Chapter 7 p. 84-97 "Clouds in the sky over a landscape, Patagonia, Argentina" © James B. Martin, Inc. / SuperStock. p. 85 "The Living Goddess" by Isabella Tree reprinted with the permission of A.P. Watt Ltd. on behalf of Isabella Tree; "Hindu goddess Durga" © iStockphoto. p. 87 Photograph of the Royal Kumari © CPImages. p. 91 Video segment "The Pursuit of Happiness" © Canadian Broadcasting Corporation; photograph © Ron Brown / SuperStock. p. 92 "The Premeditated Death of Samuel Glover" reprinted from *The Yellow Sweater and Other Stories* by Hugh Garner, Toronto, William Collins and Sons, 1953. Reprinted with permission. p. 95 Photograph courtesy of Luna Tarlo.

Chapter 8 p. 98-116 Photograph of apple © iStockphoto. p. 100 "Toggling the Switch" by Alicia Gifford first published in *Narrative Magazine* (www.narrativemagazine.com) . Copyright © 2004 by Alicia Gifford. Reprinted with permission. p. 108 Audio text "Judging When to Share Private Information" © National Public Radio. p. 110 "The Chaser" by John Collier originally appeared in the New Yorker, 1940. © 1951 by John Collier. Renewed 1978 by the estate of John Collier. Permission to reprint granted by Harold Matson Co., Inc. p. 111 "Above the City / Au-dessus de la ville" (1914-1924) by Marc Chagall (1887-1985; Russian); watercolor and gouache, Christie's Images, London, England. © Estate of Marc Chagall / SODRAC (2007). Photograph from SuperStock. p. 113 Photograph of Kate Chopin © Missouri Historical Society . p. 114 "Far Away Thoughts" by Lawrence Alma-Tadema (1836-1912; British); Christie's Images, London, England. © Christie's Images / SuperStock.

Writing Workshop 1 p. 116 "Alternative Culture" by Veena Thomas reprinted by permission of the author.

Preface

To the Student

Essays come in a variety of styles. The term *essay* can encompass everything from the humour column in a newspaper to the serious condemnation of capitalism found in a political pamphlet. Essays can, among other things, inform us, persuade us to see things differently, tell us a story, or make us laugh. Essays deal with subject matter that is, for the most part, nonfiction. Short stories, on the other hand, are developed in the imagination of the writer.

Open Road English Skills, Second Edition, includes essays and short stories that will surprise and challenge you. You will be asked to develop your critical thinking skills. An extensive Writing Workshops section will permit you to develop your writing skills.

Enjoy the open road!

To the Teacher

Open Road English Skills, Second Edition, is directed at high-intermediate to advanced students of English as a second language. *Open Road* is a comprehensive integrated skills text.

The second edition, visually enhanced in four colours, includes eight chapters focusing on contemporary themes linking reading, listening, writing, and speaking skills. High-interest readings to challenge students are in a variety of reading styles including narrative, persuasive, and informative essays, short stories, and interviews. Students develop comprehension and critical thinking skills. Audio and visual listening segments relate to the chapter contents and stimulate discussion.

After the eight chapters, you'll find five Writing Workshops. This expanded writing section provides students with strategies and extensive practice in building better essays. The final workshop gives students some specific practice on responding to fictional works. A writing checklist on the inside back cover can further aid students with their writing skills.

A new exciting feature is the Open Road Companion Website. Throughout the chapters, you'll notice links to the website where students will find activities to practise the four skills, vocabulary-building exercises, and extra information.

Complementing this book is *Open Road English Grammar*, Second Edition, which contains exercises that are based on typical student errors. Explanations are clear, and grammar exercises contain interesting biographical and historical information.

Highlights

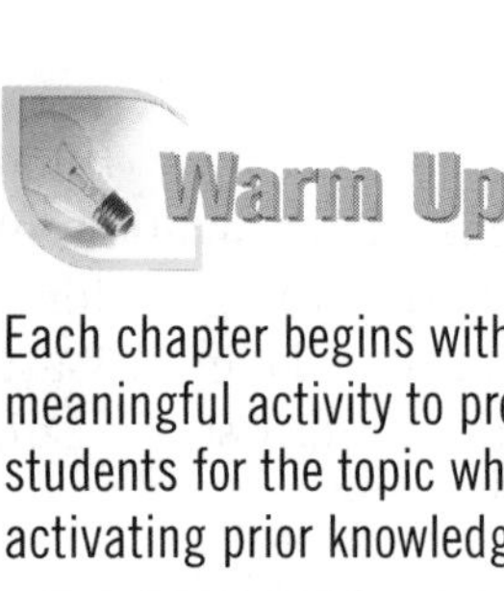

Each chapter begins with a meaningful activity to prepare students for the topic while activating prior knowledge.

Students learn strategies to improve vocabulary and read effectively.

Stimulating readings are in a variety of styles including narrative, persuasive, and informative essays, short stories, and interviews.

In each chapter, students listen to authentic interviews from CBC and NPR to expand their spoken and written expression.

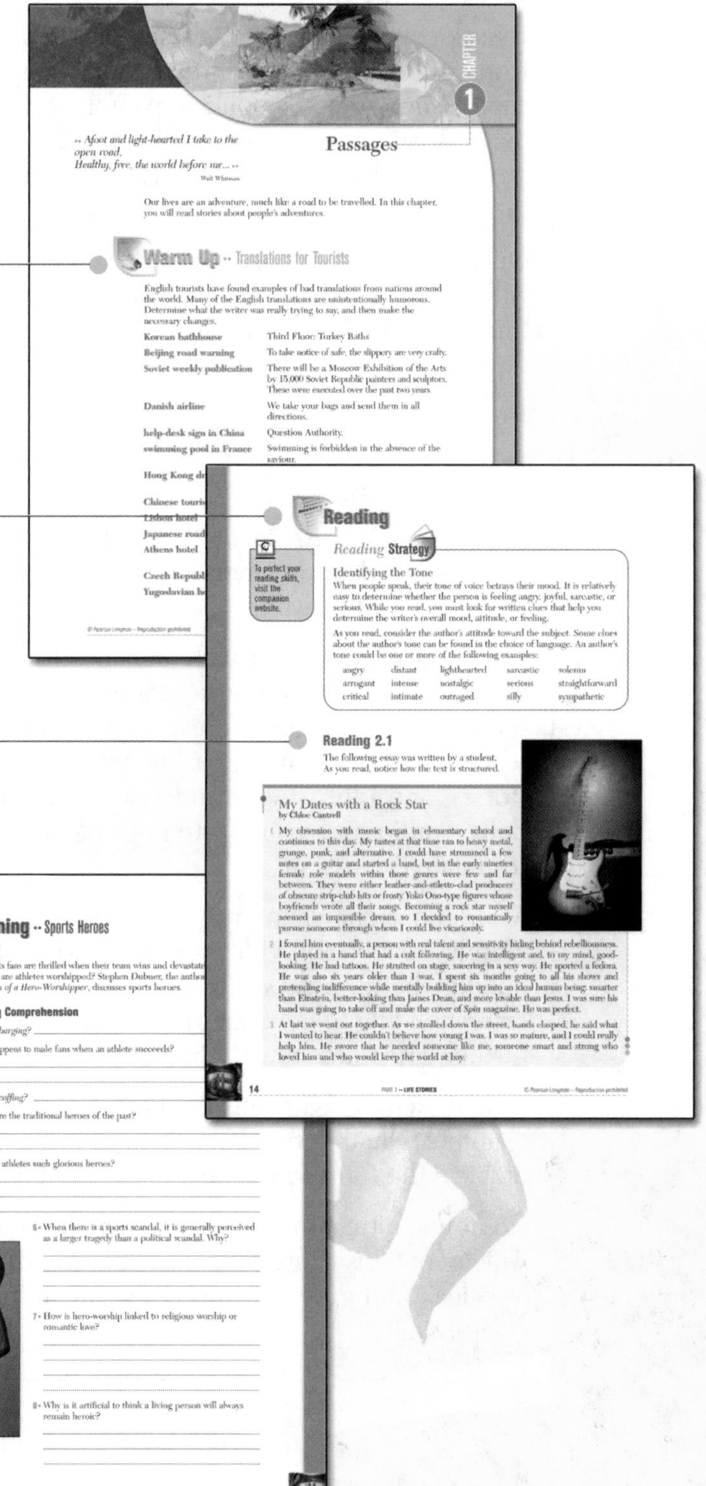

CHAPTER 1

« Afoot and light-hearted I take to the open road,
Healthy, free, the world before me... »
Walt Whitman

Passages

Our lives are an adventure, much like a road to be travelled. In this chapter, you will read stories about people's adventures.

Warm Up •• Translations for Tourists

English tourists have found examples of bad translations from nations around the world. Many of the English translations are unintentionally humorous. Determine what the writer was really trying to say, and then make the necessary changes.

Korean bathhouse	Third Floor: Turkey Baths
Beijing road warning	To take notice of safe, the slippery are very crafty.
Soviet weekly publication	There will be a Moscow Exhibition of the Arts by 15,000 Soviet Republic painters and sculptors. These were executed over the past two years.
Danish airline	We take your bags and send them in all directions.
help-desk sign in China	Question Authority.
swimming pool in France	Swimming is forbidden in the absence of the saviour.
Hong Kong dr	
Chinese touris	
Lisbon hotel	
Japanese road	
Athens hotel	
Czech Republ	
Yugoslavian h	

© Pearson Longman – Reproduction prohibited

Reading

To perfect your reading skills, visit the companion website.

Reading **Strategy**

Identifying the Tone

When people speak, their tone of voice betrays their mood. It is relatively easy to determine whether the person is feeling angry, joyful, sarcastic, or serious. While you read, you must look for written clues that help you determine the writer's overall mood, attitude, or feeling.

As you read, consider the author's attitude toward the subject. Some clues about the author's tone can be found in the choice of language. An author's tone could be one or more of the following examples:

angry	distant	lighthearted	sarcastic	solemn
arrogant	intense	nostalgic	serious	straightforward
critical	intimate	outraged	silly	sympathetic

Reading 2.1

The following essay was written by a student. As you read, notice how the text is structured.

My Dates with a Rock Star
by Chloe Cantrell

1 My obsession with music began in elementary school and continues to this day. My tastes at that time ran to heavy metal, grunge, punk, and alternative. I could have strummed a few notes on a guitar and started a band, but in the early nineties female role models within those genres were few and far between. They were either leather-and-stiletto-clad producers of obscure strip-club hits or frosty Yoko Ono-type figures whose boyfriends wrote all their songs. Becoming a rock star myself seemed an impossible dream, so I decided to romantically pursue someone through whom I could live vicariously.

2 I found him eventually, a person with real talent and sensitivity hiding behind rebelliousness. He played in a band that had a cult following. He was intelligent and, to my mind, good-looking. He had tattoos. He strutted on stage, sneering in a sexy way. He sported a fedora. He was also six years older than I was. I spent six months going to all his shows and pretending indifference while mentally building him up into an ideal human being: smarter than Einstein, better-looking than James Dean, and more lovable than Jesus. I was sure his band was going to take off and make the cover of *Spin* magazine. He was perfect.

3 At last we went out together. As we strolled down the street, hands clasped, he said what I wanted to hear. He couldn't believe how young I was. I was so mature, and I could really help him. He swore that he needed someone like me, someone smart and strong who loved him and who would keep the world at bay.

14 PART 1 •• LIFE STORIES © Pearson Longman – Reproduction prohibited

Listening •• Sports Heroes

Many sports fans are thrilled when their team wins and devastate[d when it] loses. Why are athletes worshipped? Stephen Dubner, the author [of] *Confessions of a Hero-Worshipper*, discusses sports heroes.

Listening Comprehension

1 • What is *barging*?
2 • What happens to male fans when an athlete succeeds?
3 • What is *caffing*?
4 • Who were the traditional heroes of the past?
5 • Why are athletes such glorious heroes?
6 • When there is a sports scandal, it is generally perceived as a larger tragedy than a political scandal. Why?
7 • How is hero-worship linked to religious worship or romantic love?
8 • Why is it artificial to think a living person will always remain heroic?

© Pearson Longman – Reproduction prohibited Influences •• CHAPTER 2 23

Speaking

Speaking activities ranging from discussion to interviews and presentations help students communicate confidently.

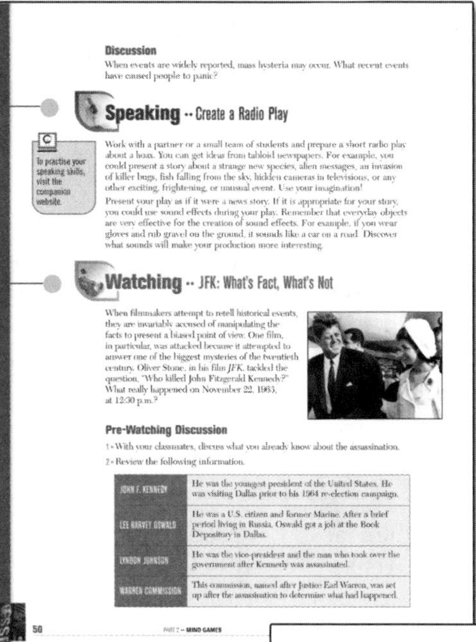

Discussion

When events are widely reported, mass hysteria may occur. What recent events have caused people to panic?

Speaking -- Create a Radio Play

To practise your speaking skills, visit the companion website.

Work with a partner or a small team of students and prepare a short radio play about a hoax. You can get ideas from tabloid newspapers. For example, you could present a story about a strange new species, alien messages, an invasion of killer bugs, fish falling from the sky, hidden cameras in televisions, or any other exciting, frightening, or unusual event. Use your imagination!

Present your play as if it were a news story. If it is appropriate for your story, you could use sound effects during your play. Remember that everyday objects are very effective for the creation of sound effects. For example, if you wear gloves and rub gravel on the ground, it sounds like a car on a road. Discover what sounds will make your production more interesting.

Watching -- JFK: What's Fact, What's Not

When filmmakers attempt to retell historical events, they are invariably accused of manipulating the facts to present a biased point of view. One film, in particular, was attacked because it attempted to answer one of the biggest mysteries of the twentieth century. Oliver Stone, in his film *JFK*, tackled the question, "Who killed John Fitzgerald Kennedy?" What really happened on November 22, 1963, at 12:30 p.m.?

Pre-Watching Discussion

1 • With your classmates, discuss what you already know about the assassination.

2 • Review the following information.

JOHN F. KENNEDY	He was the youngest president of the United States. He was visiting Dallas prior to his 1964 re-election campaign.
LEE HARVEY OSWALD	He was a U.S. citizen and former Marine. After a brief period living in Russia, Oswald got a job at the Book Depository in Dallas.
LYNDON JOHNSON	He was the vice-president and the man who took over the government after Kennedy was assassinated.
WARREN COMMISSION	This commission, named after Justice Earl Warren, was set up after the assassination to determine what had happened.

50 PART 2 -- MIND GAMES

Watching

Interesting video segments from authentic sources enrich students' understanding of content while building language skills.

"primary torturer" and said that Graner had forced him to perform acts that were against his beliefs, such as eating pork and drinking alcohol.

Other Testimony

Another soldier, Private Lynndie England, was also charged during the abuse scandal. She had posed in several of the photographs of abuse. Twenty-year-old England, who was dating Graner, said that Graner manipulated her. She apologized for her participation in the events.

Graner's mother says that her son is a "scapegoat" who would have been punished if he had refused to prepare the prisoners for interrogation. Staff Sergeant Ivan Frederick says that intelligence officers knew about the use of force and did not stop it. Two other soldiers in Graner's unit complained about the abuse of prisoners. The complaints were dismissed or ignored by senior officers.

Graner testified that what he did was "wrong" and that he "didn't enjoy it." He says that his orders were given by superiors, and that he was asked to prepare prisoners for interrogation: "We were asked to do certain things that I wasn't trained to do." Graner contends that he was obeying orders from military intelligence to weaken the prisoners and prepare them for interrogation.

The prosecution argues that Graner determined the type of abuse and that he appeared to enjoy punching and humiliating prisoners, as is shown in photos of him smiling over bleeding and naked detainees. The prosecution also points out that even if Graner were following orders from senior officers, he should have known that the orders were illegal.

Is Charles Graner guilty?
If so, what should his sentence be?

Sources: CNN.com
"Family Defends Soldier" by Dennis B. Roddy, Pittsburgh Post-Gazette;
"3 to Be Arraigned" by Christian Davenport and Michael Amon, Washington Post;
National Public Radio

Writing Topics

Challenging writing topics allow students to practise different writing patterns and integrate content.

Writing Topics

To review some of the vocabulary studied in this chapter, visit the companion website.

Write a composition about one of the following topics. Remember to include a thesis statement and provide supporting examples. Before handing in your work, refer to the Writing Checklist on the inside back cover.

1 • What causes wars? Think of two or three reasons why countries engage in wars.

2 • Describe a moment that changed the world. Explain some ways it has impacted people in your society.

3 • What do the Milgram Experiment and the Stanford Prison Experiment tell us about human aggression?

4 • Is killing acceptable when someone wears a military uniform? You can refer to "Conscience."

5 • When soldiers commit war crimes, is the defence of "I was following orders" legitimate? Why or why not? You might think about examples, such as when some soldiers in Iraq's Abu Ghraib prison tortured detainees.

6 • Why is history important? What can we learn from the past?

© Pearson Longman – Reproduction prohibited Conscience -- CHAPTER 6 83

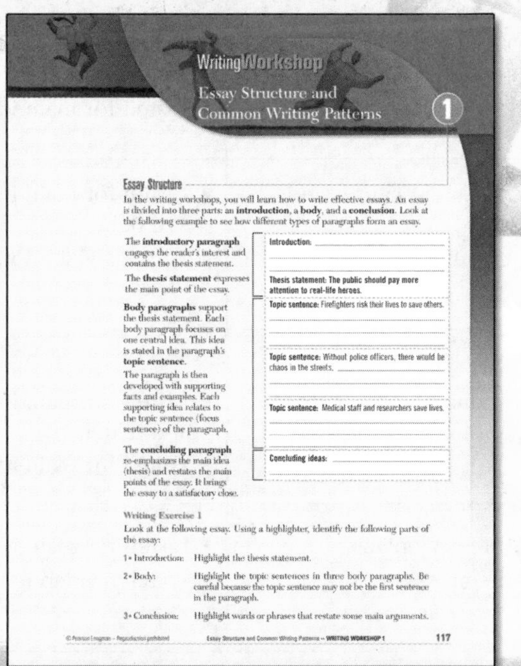

WritingWorkshop

Essay Structure and Common Writing Patterns 1

Essay Structure

In the writing workshops, you will learn how to write effective essays. An essay is divided into three parts: an **introduction**, a **body**, and a **conclusion**. Look at the following example to see how different types of paragraphs form an essay.

The **introductory paragraph** engages the reader's interest and contains the thesis statement.

The **thesis statement** expresses the main point of the essay.

Body paragraphs support the thesis statement. Each body paragraph focuses on one central idea. This idea is stated in the paragraph's **topic sentence**.

The paragraph is then developed with supporting facts and examples. Each supporting idea relates to the topic sentence (focus sentence) of the paragraph.

The **concluding paragraph** re-emphasizes the main idea (thesis) and restates the main points of the essay. It brings the essay to a satisfactory close.

Introduction: ____________

Thesis statement: The public should pay more attention to real-life heroes.

Topic sentence: Firefighters risk their lives to save others.

Topic sentence: Without police officers, there would be chaos in the streets.

Topic sentence: Medical staff and researchers save lives.

Concluding ideas: ____________

Writing Exercise 1

Look at the following essay. Using a highlighter, identify the following parts of the essay:

1 • Introduction: Highlight the thesis statement.

2 • Body: Highlight the topic sentences in three body paragraphs. Be careful because the topic sentence may not be the first sentence in the paragraph.

3 • Conclusion: Highlight words or phrases that restate some main arguments.

© Pearson Longman – Reproduction prohibited Essay Structure and Common Writing Patterns -- WRITING WORKSHOP 1 117

Extensions and practice activities help students consolidate what they have learned.

Five writing workshops provide students with strategies and extensive practice to build better essays.

Scope and Sequence

	READING	WRITING	LISTENING/WATCHING
PART 1: LIFE STORIES			
CHAPTER 1 **Passages**	• Use context clues to understand vocabulary • Identify main ideas	• Write short responses • Write using description and narration • Develop an argument	• Listen for main and supporting ideas
CHAPTER 2 **Influences**	• Identify the tone • Use context clues • Identify main and supporting ideas	• Support an argument • Write using comparison and contrast	• Listen for main and supporting ideas • Interpret messages in a video
PART 2: MIND GAMES			
CHAPTER 3 **Dealing with Differences**	• Recognize bias • Identify subjective and objective writing • Do team reading	• Write interview questions • Write an essay • Summarize main ideas • Make an arts survey	• Listen for main ideas • Watch a video for main ideas • Understand everyday language
CHAPTER 4 **The Age of Persuasion**	• Determine audience and purpose • Identify cognates	• Write questions • Write a paragraph based on a partner's responses • Write an essay	• Listen for main ideas • Watch a video • Identify biographical information
PART 3: INNOCENCE AND GUILT			
CHAPTER 5 **The Memory Wars**	• Learn summarizing • Identify plagiarism	• Write a summary • Write types of essays	• Watch for ideas and make inferences • Listen for main ideas
CHAPTER 6 **Conscience**	• Scan for information • Recognize irony • Identify main ideas and understand details	• Write about causes and effects • Argue a point	• Listen for main ideas and details • Watch a video for main ideas
PART 4: VALUES			
CHAPTER 7 **Searching**	• Consider the context • Identify figurative devices	• Respond to a short story • Write types of essays	• Listen for main ideas and details • Watch for main ideas
CHAPTER 8 **Ethics**	• Scan for information • Make inferences	• Write essay plans • Write an essay	• Listen for main ideas • Watch a video for main ideas

SPEAKING	VOCABULARY	CRITICAL THINKING
• Share information • Present a personal story • Discuss proverbs and poor translations	• Learn descriptive words • Understand specific verbs	• Express opinions • Analyze outcomes
• Discuss with a team • Present an influential individual	• Understand idiomatic expressions • Identify vivid verbs	• Consider differing views • Analyze motives
• Present an issue • Ask and answer questions • Discuss stereotypes	• Develop synonyms • Understand commonly confused words	• Recognize bias • Draw inferences • Determine subjectivity
• Ask and answer questions • Discuss advertising • Pronounce past tense verbs	• Identify terms • Infer meanings • Interpret nature versus nurture arguments	• Make inferences • Analyze events
• Use descriptive language • Discuss issues	• Learn descriptive vocabulary • Learn synonyms	• Interpret manipulation techniques • Make moral decisions
• Discuss historical events • Discuss issues • Debate a military court case	• Learn commonly confused words • Use synonyms	• Interpret motives • Analyze facts • Debate issues
• Discuss spiritual beliefs • Describe common objects	• Learn descriptive vocabulary • Use terms in context	• Justify courses of action • Make moral decisions
• Discuss issues • Present an ethical dilemma	• Learn short story vocabulary	• Interpret motivations • Defend a position

Table of Contents

Open Road English Skills, Second Edition

PART 3: INNOCENCE AND GUILT

PART 4: VALUES

WRITING WORKSHOPS

CHAPTER 1

Passages

Afoot and light-hearted I take to the open road,
Healthy, free, the world before me...

Walt Whitman

Our lives are an adventure, much like a road to be travelled. In this chapter, you will read stories about people's adventures.

Warm Up •• Translations for Tourists

English tourists have found examples of bad translations from nations around the world. Many of the English translations are unintentionally humorous. Determine what the writer was really trying to say, and then make the necessary changes.

Korean bathhouse	Third Floor: Turkey Baths
Beijing road warning	To take notice of safe, the slippery are very crafty.
Soviet weekly publication	There will be a Moscow Exhibition of the Arts by 15,000 Soviet Republic painters and sculptors. These were executed over the past two years.
Danish airline	We take your bags and send them in all directions.
help-desk sign in China	Question Authority.
swimming pool in France	Swimming is forbidden in the absence of the saviour.
Hong Kong dress shop	Because is big rush we will execute customers in strict rotation.
Chinese tourist shop	Keep this candle out of children.
Lisbon hotel	Please deposit your values at the front desk.
Japanese road sign	Hard times up ahead.
Athens hotel	Visitors are expected to complain at the office between the hours of 9 and 11 a.m. daily.
Czech Republic zoo	No smoothen the lion.
Yugoslavian hotel	The flattening of underwear with pleasure is the job of the chambermaid.

To perfect your reading skills, visit the companion website.

Japanese detour sign	Stop. Drive sideways.
Bangkok temple	It is forbidden to enter a woman even a foreigner if dressed like a man.

Reading

Reading Strategy

Using Context Clues

Often, the meaning of a particular word or expression can be guessed at when you examine the context in which it is being used. Use the following strategy when you see an unfamiliar word:

1• Look at the word.
Is it a noun, a verb, or an adjective? Knowing how the word functions in the sentence can help you guess its meaning.

2• Look at the parts of the word.
Identify prefixes and suffixes to help you find the meaning of a word. For example, the prefixes *un-*, *dis-*, and *il-* mean "not," the prefix *multi-* means "many," and the suffix *-less* means "without."

3• Look at surrounding words.
Look at the entire sentence and try to see how the difficult word relates to those surrounding it. There may be a synonym (word that means the same thing) or an antonym (word that means the opposite) or other terms in the sentence that can help define the word.

4• Look at surrounding sentences.
Sometimes you can guess the meaning of a difficult word by looking at the sentences, paragraphs, and punctuation marks surrounding it. When you use logic, the meaning becomes clear.

In most cases, you can guess the meaning of a new word by combining your own knowledge of the topic with the information conveyed in the words and phrases surrounding the difficult word.

Reading Exercise

Can you define the words *baffled, strewn, fume*, and *haven*? __________

Perhaps you aren't quite sure. Looking at the words in context makes it much easier to guess their definitions.

> When I arrived in my hometown, I was **baffled** by the changes in my old neighbourhood. Garbage was **strewn** across front lawns, paint peeled on the greying wooden homes, and roofs sagged. The auto body shop on the corner emanated horrible **fumes** of turpentine and paint, forcing me to cover my nose when I passed it. I wondered what had happened to my former safe **haven**.

Now write your own definition of the words as they are used in the context.

baffled ____________________ strewn ____________________

fume ____________________ haven ____________________

Reading 1.1

The international travel writer Arthur Frommer has written extensively about his experiences. In the following text, Frommer explains what travelling has taught him. As you read about his experiences, use context clues to guess the meanings of the words in red. Write your definitions in the spaces provided. The first one has been done for you.

How Travel Has Changed My Life

by Arthur Frommer

Write definitions

1 To nearly a hundred countries, for millions and millions of miles, I've travelled for more than forty years, and I am a different person because of it. On every trip to everywhere, in unfamiliar **surroundings**, among new and different people, our consciousness changes and we develop new beliefs such as the following. *environments*

2 **We are all alike.** I am in the dark dung hut of a Maasai family in eastern Africa. Through an interpreter, the woman of the house tells me that she hopes to learn to read. And why? So she can study a handbook on properly raising children. I am sitting cross-legged on a tatami mat in the apartment of a young Japanese couple. Their daughter, they tell me, is complaining about the **harshness** of her first-grade teacher. ____________

3 Travel has taught me that despite all the exotic differences of dress and language, of political and religious beliefs, all the world's people are essentially alike. We all have the same urges and concerns; we all **yearn for** the same goals. And those who patronize other people, or demonize those with whom they disagree, or regard them as funny or backward, are foolish, indeed; they have not yet learned the lessons of travel. ____________

4 **We all think ourselves virtuous.** At the bar of an Amsterdam café, I am talking with a Dutch friend. Last night, he tells me, a nationwide telethon raised the equivalent of about forty million dollars for cancer research. "Only in Holland," he says, "could such results be obtained."

5 We all think ourselves the best, and we all believe with great sincerity in the superiority of our own nation and culture, as compared with others. We have all heard politicians proclaim this nation or that nation to be the finest on earth. Travel has rid me of that **smug** chauvinism; it exposes me to the finest in every land, and makes me distinctly uneasy when I later return home and hear people proclaiming their own nation to be better than others. ____________

6 **We are all responsible for one another.** It is the early 1980s. Dancing down a broad boulevard of Zagreb comes a succession of laughing, gaily-clad groups gathered there for a nationwide folk-dance festival of Yugoslavia. At the **curb**, I stand watching Muslims, Christians, Bosnians, Croatians, and Serbs celebrating in complete harmony. In later years, and because of travel, I remember them as distinct physical presences, not as abstractions; I get physically ill when I read of the violence between them. I feel the same intimate bond with the Protestants and Catholics of Northern Ireland, whose cities I visited at the height of the "troubles," and with people of both Egypt and Israel, to which I once led groups of tourists. Travel makes it impossible to pay no **heed** to the sufferings of others, simply because they are far away; it erases distance, and makes us more sensitive citizens of the world, yearning for peace everywhere.

7 **We grow when we confront our political or religious opposites.** I am at a residential yoga community, opening my mind to non-linear thinking. And though the guru's speech is directly at odds with my usual rationalism, I find myself enjoying it and savouring this clash of new ideas. Another time I am at a "personal growth centre" on the West Coast, in a class of "encounter therapy." I am told that I must **clasp** hands with the elderly gentleman opposite me, look deeply into his eyes, wish him well, and give him a bear hug. Though I am initially loath to do so, I then feel a surge of shame that I have allowed myself to be so emotionally controlled that I cannot offer sympathy to a fellow human being.

8 Travel exposes us to ideas, lifestyles, theologies, and philosophies that challenge our most cherished beliefs. It takes us out of a setting in which everyone thinks the same, and sends us into the unknown, to our political or religious adversaries. Travel has made me confront my "opposites."

9 **More than a single answer exists for human problems.** I am walking the streets of Hong Kong, past signs for herbal medicines and acupuncturists. And all around are millions of people perfectly content with these approaches to personal health so different from our own. Another time I am lying in a copper bathtub filled with naturally-carbonated water, in a baths establishment of the Belgian city of Spa. And though my mind tells me it can't be, that this reliance on "water cures" is scientific **rubbish**, I feel something happening to my body, and begin to suspect that the three hundred million Europeans who believe in such remedies may not be wrong.

10 Travel teaches that a whole range of unusual practices may work in differing contexts; it suggests new approaches for our own society, and it keeps us open to novel proposals and experiments in every field.

11 **All people should be "minorities."** I walk the great cities of China, and gradually realize that in their midst, I am a minority in the same way that others are minorities in the city where I live. And I feel, as so many other travellers have felt, the gradual weakening of whatever racist impulses still inhabit my subconscious. Travel teaches the absurdity of reacting to people according to their colour. It makes everyone a minority on occasion. And people who come back from such trips are often changed by the experience, as I have been.

12 Travel, for many, is a mere recreation. But travel is also education, perhaps the best form of education. Certainly, it impacts the mind in a way that sometimes no other activity—even that of widespread reading—can quite do. It has changed my life and made me a different sort of person.

13 We are the first generation in human history to be able to travel to other continents as easily as we once took a trolley to the next town. Dare we hope that a more understanding, more tolerant, and more peaceful individual will be brought about by that development?

Comprehension •• Find Main and Supporting Ideas

1 • How is the author an authority on this subject? ______________________

____

2 • Using your own words, sum up the author's main point.

____

____

3 • How does the author support his main point? ______________________

____

4 • Underline the areas of the world the author mentions in this essay.

Asia	South America	North America
Africa	Europe	Australia

5 • In Paragraph 12, Frommer writes that travel has "made me a different sort of person." How has travel changed his character? Think of four answers.

____

____

____

____

____

To work on your writing skills, visit the companion website.

Listening •• Travel Stories from Syria

Heather Burles got the travel bug and went to the ancient city of Damascus, Syria. Despite the culture shock, and, at times, dangerous situations, Heather returned with a new appreciation for that foreign land. She has written a book about her experiences called *Smoldering Incense, Hammered Brass*. In an interview for CBC Radio, Heather discusses her journey.

Listening Comprehension

Answer the following questions.

1 • In Canada, what kind of work did Heather do? ______________________

____

2 • Why did Heather go to Syria? ______________________

____

3 • Why did Heather decide to get a one-way ticket? ______________________

____

4 • What happened when she arrived at her hotel? ______________________

____

____

____

5 • Heather said that she had very few problems as a single woman travelling in Syria. What two things did she do to minimize the chances of having problems?

____

____

6 • She did have problems with some men. Who were they, and why did they treat her differently?

____

____

7 • According to Heather, why do some Syrian men think that Western women are amoral?

____

____

8 • When Heather's boyfriend came to Syria, how did Heather present him to people?

____

9 • How did men treat Heather differently when her boyfriend was in Syria?

____

____

____

10 • Heather was at a Bedouin feast and she was offered sheep's tongue. How did she handle the situation?

____

____

Reading

Reading 1.2

Rob Penn left a decent job working in a London law office to ride his bike around the world. Today, he writes and photographs for a number of leading London publications including *The Times* and *Condé Nast Traveller*. As you read about his experiences, use context clues to guess the meanings of the words in red. Write your definitions in the spaces provided. The first one has been done for you.

The Longest Ride
by Rob Penn

Write definitions

1 About an hour after the crash—I had come over the handlebars flying downhill on a gravel road—the blood on my face and in my hair had **congealed**. Sweat was running off my forehead, and my ripped T-shirt hung off one shoulder. I leaned my bike against the gate of a farm, the first building I had seen since the morning, and walked up the drive. Children and women scattered, shrieking, and the farmer, a barrel-chested Kyrgyz man with taut, Mongoloid features, appeared from the shadows with a pistol at the end of his stiff arm. *hardened*

2 *"Dobriy dyen'. Kag dyela?"* I said. There was no reply, but his eyes **flicked** past me to the gate and my bicycle. At once, the pistol arm fell limp and the leathery brown skin on his face reset to a broad grin. Ten minutes later, I was eating kebabs and yogourt as two girls sponged my brow. Once again, I had my bicycle to thank for my salvation. ______________

3 In the three years it took me to ride 24,000 miles round the world, I was frequently amazed at the genuine and unmistakable trust people from the thirty-one countries I crossed placed in me, simply because I was riding a bicycle. On a practical level, trust leads to food and accommodation, but it is also a key to kinship and understanding. And in modern times, when

we can be at least **cursorily** familiar with so much of the planet from an armchair, this is one of the greatest goals of travel. ____________

4 Not that I knew this when I set off from New York in 1995. Having ground my existence to a lifeless uniformity working in London as a city solicitor, I was after adventure plain and simple. I chose to travel by bicycle by default—I could not ride a horse, walking was too slow, a four-wheel drive was too expensive, and I had heard too many "worst bus journey I ever had" **yarns** to contemplate public transport. ____________

5 To my advantage and delight, I discovered that there is something virtuous in a bicycle. As Dorothy L. Sayers wrote, "You can't imagine a bicyclist committing a crime, can you?" Certainly, no sane thief would use one for his **getaway**. ____________ But it is also a ubiquitous mode of transport used by the rich and the poor. People know well of the physical effort involved, and it is this hardship that raises the status of cyclist from traveller to pilgrim. Only a fraction of the world's people can afford to travel exclusively for pleasure, but pilgrimage is a feature of all the world's religions. No matter where I was in the world, I was fortunate to find a measure of empathy with the locals.

6 Happy memories do stick more strongly, but to suggest that the entire journey was **a breeze** and an indulgence of humanity's largesse would be wrong. ____________ I was robbed three times (two further attempted robberies I managed to bungle my way out of), arrested twice—in Sri Lanka and Uzbekistan—and stoned by children in both hemispheres.

7 Yet what really **roused** my courage were my own mistakes, which I rode into with a dangerous combination of innocence and arrogance. ____________ I ran out of food and water in the Australian outback because I got drunk and failed to add up the miles to the next town correctly. I rode through the cauldron of central India in searing pre-monsoon heat, got dysentery, lost my appetite, carried on riding, and then physically collapsed. I reached eastern Turkey and the central Anatolian plateau in January and had to endure days when the temperature never rose above minus five degrees. With the wind chill, my hands and feet were painfully cold, and I had to beg and force my way into homes, garages, and police stations to warm up. It was miserable.

8 I entered Iran on a five-day transit visa, and to extend it I had to do battle with base apparatchiks in five different "Alien Bureaus." When I lost my temper in the Tehran office, I was **flung** onto the pavement by the scruff of my neck to the amusement of a throng of Afghans waiting for work permits. ____________

9 In Kosovo, I wrote in my diary the address of an Albanian family to send them a photo. The following day, at a Serbian military checkpoint, soldiers read this and, thinking that I was working for, or at least a sympathiser with, the Kosovo Liberation Army, tore open my bags and interrogated me. I was in Kosovo against everybody's good advice, and I felt exposed and foolish.

10 It took the Serbian soldiers some time to get over the shock of seeing me there on a bicycle. But I was used to this sort of consternation. In fact, I had used these stunned moments to **bluff** my way over a number of borders in China, Uzbekistan, Iran, and Syria. Furthermore, I never had to pay a bribe. I felt that if I had arrived at these deserted border posts, manned by indolent soldiers, in a Land Cruiser, I would have been handing out crisp **greenbacks** faster than you can say, "What special tax?"

11 Life on a bicycle is very earnest, ascetic even. The simplest things such as washing, eating, and reading a book became luxuries for me. This asceticism, combined with the physical exertion and, of course, the solitude, made me a more sensitized and, I believe, more perceptive traveller. However, the manner in which I adapted, albeit slowly, to life on the road made arriving home after three years more difficult than the greatest challenges of the trip. I was, I discovered, more adept at dealing with gun-toting, brawny Kyrgyz farmers than I was at making conversation with London co-workers.

Comprehension

1 • Penn begins his essay with a story about an event that occurred in Kyrgyzstan.What is Penn's main point in Paragraphs 1 and 2?

2 • Why does Penn say that he travelled on a bicycle "by default"?

3 • How does the status of a traveller change when he or she arrives on a bicycle instead of in a car, bus, train, or plane?

4 • In Paragraph 5, Penn writes, "to suggest that the entire journey was a breeze and an indulgence of humanity's largesse would be wrong." Why does he say this?

5 • Penn says that he made mistakes as a result of his innocence and arrogance. What examples show arrogance?

____

____

____

6 • In Paragraph 11, why does Penn call travelling by bicycle "ascetic"?

____

7 • What is the main idea of the essay? In one sentence, how would you describe this essay to someone else? Your statement of main idea should contain the answers to such questions as *who*, *what*, *when*, *where*, *why*, and *how*.

____

____

____

Looking at Language

8 • List the four irregular simple past tense verbs in Paragraph 9.

__________ __________ __________ __________

9 • In Paragraph 9, why is the verb *was working* in the past progressive tense?

____

____

Part 1: Proverbs and Quotations

A proverb is a popular saying that expresses a basic truth about life. It often offers advice or a warning. Read the following proverbs. If any proverb is unclear, discuss it with your classmates and restate it in your own words.

- Every cloud has a silver lining. (English proverb)
- The squeaky wheel gets the grease. (Unknown origin)
- Don't cross a bridge until you come to it. (English proverb)
- Half a loaf is better than none. (English proverb)
- A lie travels farther than the truth. (Irish proverb)
- A jack of all trades is a master of none. (English proverb)
- Let sleeping dogs lie. (English proverb)
- You cannot unscramble eggs. (North American proverb)
- It is better to wear out shoes than sheets. (Scottish proverb)
- Those who cannot remember the past are condemned to repeat it. (George Santayana, Spanish poet and philosopher)

To develop your listening skills, visit the companion website.

- An eye for an eye leads to a world of the blind. (Mahatma Gandhi)
- If I had to live my life over again, I would make the same mistakes, only sooner. (Tallulah Bankhead)
- A goal without a plan is just a wish. (Antoine de Saint-Exupéry)

Part 2: Present a Life Experience

Prepare a presentation about an experience that changed your life. If you have trouble coming up with ideas, ask yourself the following questions:

- Have I ever done something really positive (forgiven someone, helped someone, stopped taking someone for granted, and so on) or really negative (cheated, lied, excluded someone, ridiculed someone, and so on)?
- Has anyone near me ever had an experience that taught me a lesson?
- Has any story, movie, or real-life news event had a profound impact on me and changed me in some way?

Structure

1. Explain what happened.
2. Explain how the event changed your life or the life of someone you know.
3. Conclude with a proverb or quotation. You can choose one from the previous list, or find your own quotation. Visit the companion website for links to quotation sites.

Points to Remember

- Your presentation should be three to five minutes in length.
- You may use cue cards that contain up to fifteen key words. Do not read your text!
- Make sure that your verbs are correctly formed and pronounced.
- Practise your presentation but don't memorize it. (If you recite a memorized text, it can sound very unnatural.)

Tip Grammar

Pronunciation of Regular Past Tense Verbs

- When the verb ends in *t* or *d*, pronounce the final *-ed* as a separate syllable.

  wanted [want id] started [start id] guarded [gard id]
- When the verb ends in a voiced sound, the final *ed* is pronounced *d*.

  lived [livd] boiled [boild] called [cald]
- When the verb ends in a voiceless sound (*sh, ch, k, p, s, or x*), the final *-ed* sounds like a *t*.

  asked [askt] marched [marcht] baked [baykt]

Pronunciation of Verbs Ending in *ght*

- When irregular past tense verbs end in *ght*, the *gh* is silent. Only pronounce the final *t*.

  taught [tot] bought [bot] thought [thot]

To practise pronouncing past tense verbs, visit the companion website.

Writing Topics

Write a composition about one of the following topics. Remember to include a thesis statement and provide supporting examples. Before handing in your work, refer to the Writing Checklist on the inside back cover.

1 • "Two roads diverged in a wood, and I—I took the one less travelled by, and that has made all the difference." *Robert Frost, poet*
Respond to the quotation. Write an essay explaining how something—it could be a proud moment, a bad decision, a mistake, or a shocking event—made a difference in your life.

2 • Give advice to travellers. What should they do when they plan and go on a trip?

3 • Choose a photograph from your past. Describe what was happening when the picture was taken. Use descriptive words and phrases. (For more information about descriptive writing, see page 119 of Writing Workshop 1.)

4 • Write an essay about mistakes. First, narrow your topic. You might write about mistakes made by first-year college students or by first-time travellers. Develop your topic with at least two supporting points, adding examples and anecdotes to support each point.

To review some of the vocabulary studied in this chapter, visit the companion website.

Use Vivid Language

After you have made the first draft of your essay, reread it. Then identify five common overused verbs. Replace each verb with a more vivid and specific verb.

First draft: When he walks onstage, the crowd looks at him with awe.

Revision: When he strolls onstage, the crowd gazes adoringly at him.

CHAPTER 2

Influences

•• It is better to deserve honours and not have them than to have them and not deserve them. ••

Mark Twain

Can you think of a person we honour who is not deserving of that honour? This chapter explores contemporary individuals who may or may not be heroic.

Warm Up •• Talking about Heroes

Join a group of students and discuss the following questions. When it is your turn to talk, read the question out loud and then answer it with the first ideas that come to mind. Try to talk without stopping.

1 • Which fields or jobs get the most respect? Think of at least five fields. Explain why.

2 • Which fields or jobs get the least respect? Think of at least five fields. Explain why.

3 • Past heroes were politicians and military figures. How are politicians and military officials viewed today? Give examples.

4 • Why do people idolize actors and singers?

5 • During childhood, who do we idolize? Think about television and movie heroes.

6 • During adolescence and adulthood, how do our heroes change?

7 • Pablo Picasso neglected his children, and he was cruel to some of his mistresses. Should it matter if an icon has a dark side?

8 • Do we idolize different traits in men and women? Give examples of famous males and females.

9 • Some well-known people have been famously misquoted. For example, Marie Antoinette never actually said, "Let them eat cake." Why would such a misquotation endure?

Reading

To perfect your reading skills, visit the companion website.

Reading Strategy

Identifying the Tone

When people speak, their tone of voice betrays their mood. It is relatively easy to determine whether the person is feeling angry, joyful, sarcastic, or serious. While you read, you must look for written clues that help you determine the writer's overall mood, attitude, or feeling.

As you read, consider the author's attitude toward the subject. Some clues about the author's tone can be found in the choice of language. An author's tone could be one or more of the following examples:

angry	distant	lighthearted	sarcastic	solemn
arrogant	intense	nostalgic	serious	straightforward
critical	intimate	outraged	silly	sympathetic

Reading 2.1

The following essay was written by a student. As you read, notice how the text is structured.

My Dates with a Rock Star

by Chloe Cantrell

1 My obsession with music began in elementary school and continues to this day. My tastes at that time ran to heavy metal, grunge, punk, and alternative. I could have strummed a few notes on a guitar and started a band, but in the early nineties female role models within those genres were few and far between. They were either leather-and-stiletto-clad producers of obscure strip-club hits or frosty Yoko Ono-type figures whose boyfriends wrote all their songs. Becoming a rock star myself seemed an impossible dream, so I decided to romantically pursue someone through whom I could live vicariously.

2 I found him eventually, a person with real talent and sensitivity hiding behind rebelliousness. He played in a band that had a cult following. He was intelligent and, to my mind, good-looking. He had tattoos. He strutted on stage, sneering in a sexy way. He sported a fedora. He was also six years older than I was. I spent six months going to all his shows and pretending indifference while mentally building him up into an ideal human being: smarter than Einstein, better-looking than James Dean, and more lovable than Jesus. I was sure his band was going to take off and make the cover of *Spin* magazine. He was perfect.

3 At last we went out together. As we strolled down the street, hands clasped, he said what I wanted to hear. He couldn't believe how young I was. I was so mature, and I could really help him. He swore that he needed someone like me, someone smart and strong who loved him and who would keep the world at bay.

4 His flaws began to show early on, I must admit. One night after he had imbibed a staggering number of beers, he mumbled a few remarks that made me see him in a slightly different light. "I don't know what it is about really young girls," he shrugged. "The only problem is I lose interest fast and I need a new one." The next day, I reminded him of what he had said, and he informed me sorrowfully that although he was likely to tire of me before long, I wasn't to take it personally. Patting my hand, he suggested that we would always remain friends.

5 I tried to swallow the pill and appreciate his benevolent offer of eternal friendship, but I couldn't quite. The trouble was I was still smitten. I kept going to his shows, though I began noticing that he often made mistakes onstage, causing his bandmates to glare at him furiously. We still went out, though he had dropped the pretence of being my boyfriend. He explained that he had a fear of commitment, though when he staggered and slurred his words, I observed that he didn't have trouble committing to a bottle of Jack Daniels. His fedora still looked cool, but when it came off, I could no longer overlook his prematurely but drastically receding hairline.

6 Finally there was a horrible night when I arrived late at a party at his house and found him asleep in bed with another girl—a girl who was not particularly pretty, intelligent, or charming, but who was a year younger than I was. As I sat in the living room unsuccessfully hiding my misery, the drummer from his band crouched beside me and tried to comfort me. It would have helped more if he hadn't been stroking my thigh. I shoved his hand away and left the party. I also left my musician's life.

7 He made a few half-hearted attempts to reach me. When we spoke, he apologized. He reiterated his intention to be my friend, but I was feeling far from friendly myself. I rejoiced on hearing that he had been kicked out of his band. I could see him clearly now for what he was: a second-rate musician, weak in life and love. His alcoholism was a disease, not an eccentricity. His proclivity for young women was just another symptom of insecurity. But my feelings had been genuine, if deluded, and beyond wounded pride, I was heartbroken. I swore I would never again mistake an ideal for a person.

Vocabulary and Comprehension

1. Underline the thesis statement. The thesis statement is the sentence that sums up the main idea of the essay.
2. In Paragraph 1, the author says that she wanted to meet a guy through whom she could "live vicariously." What does she mean?

   ____

   ____
3. Find a word in Paragraph 5 that means "infatuated." ______________
4. In Paragraph 5, the author writes, "I tried to swallow the pill." What "pill" was she referring to?

   ____
5. In Paragraph 7, what is the meaning of "proclivity"? ______________
6. In Paragraph 7, the author says that she was deluded. How was she deluded?

   ____

   ____

7 • What are some stereotyped ideas about rock stars? ___

___

8 • What were some of the rock star's flaws? ___

___

9 • In Paragraph 4, the author admits that the rock star's character flaws showed early on. For instance, he admitted that he likes young girls. Why do you think she kept dating him?

___

___

10 • What is the author's tone? You can have more than one answer. (For a definition of tone, see the Reading Strategy that precedes this essay.)

delighted	intense	solemn	sarcastic	outraged
distant	reflective	apologetic	forgiving	bitter

Vocabulary Boost (Team Activity)

The verbs listed below appeared in the essay, "My Date with a Rock Star." Form a group of three students. You must each choose a column. Using context clues and a dictionary, determine what the words in your column mean. (The paragraph number is indicated in parentheses.) Be prepared to act out each verb for your partners.

A	B	C
strum (1)	swear (3)	glare (5)
strut (2)	imbibe (4)	stagger (5)
sneer (2)	mumble (4)	slur (5)
sport (2)	shrug (4)	crouch (6)
stroll (3)	pat (4)	stroke (6)
clasp (3)	swallow (5)	shove (6)

Discussion or Written Response

1 • Why do people elevate rock stars, athletes, actors, and other celebrities to such a high status? What do celebrities represent?

2 • What are the positive or negative effects of our celebrity culture?

To work on your writing skills, visit the companion website.

Grammar

Affect vs. *Effect*

Affect is a verb that means "to influence or change." *Effect* is a noun that means "the result."

Verb: How does an act of heroism **affect** a person?

Noun: The news had an interesting **effect** on the viewers.

Watching •• The Hero among Us

The essay "My Date with a Rock Star" explores idol worship in our celebrity-focused culture. But what is the definition of a true hero? The video segment explores average people who, when confronted with a crisis, risk their lives to save others. Scan the following questions before you watch the video segment.

Comprehension

1 • What is the title of Professor Michael Lessie's book? ____________________

2 • According to Professor Lessie, what do we learn from heroes of mythology?

____

3 • According to Professor Lessie, what do real-life heroes teach us? ____________

____

4 • Are we all capable of heroism? Explain. ____________________

____

5 • What is Major Jalbert's strategy during a crisis?

a) Stop and think and see what you can do. **b)** Act first, think later.

6 • Several heroic individuals are profiled. Write the letter of the heroic act next to the person who performed that act.

INDIVIDUAL		HEROIC ACTION
1. Anna Lang	______	a. ran into a burning house and saved the children
2. Steve Lopez	______	b. befriended a hijacker so that the passengers could be saved
3. Mary Dewey	______	c. swam through burning water to save a child
4. David Chevarie	______	d. jumped onto a subway track to save a suicidal woman

7 • Why did the young man jump onto the subway tracks?

a) He knew and trusted his own youth and fitness.

b) He knew he could help the woman.

c) He didn't want to spend the rest of his life thinking, "I could have done something."

d) All of the above

8 • Why would the engineering student probably not jump onto subway tracks to save someone again?

____

____

9 • According to Professor Lessie, what motivated the woman who swam through burning water?

a) Instinct. She didn't think about it.

b) A guilty conscience. She was the driver of the vehicle that fell off the bridge.

c) Glory. She wanted recognition for her act.

10 • When the woman in the burning water yelled for help to a man on the shore, the man simply ignored her. According to Professor Lessie,

a) the man's inaction was common. b) the man's inaction was uncommon.

11 • The stewardess chose to stay on the plane with the hijacker. Why did she make that choice?

____

____

12 • What happens to heroes after their feats of courage, according to Professor Lessie?

____

____

Discussion or Written Response

1 • The man on the shore ignored a woman's screams for help. Why did he ignore her? What causes some people to ignore such cries for help?

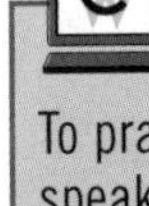

To practise your speaking skills, visit the companion website.

2 • The friends and family of the young electrical-engineering student think that he should never have jumped onto the subway tracks. Remember that the film also mentions many people who died during acts of heroism. Do you think that the young man acted more recklessly than the other heroes? Explain your answer.

3 • Of the five individuals mentioned in the video, which one acted in the most selfless, heroic manner? Explain your answer.

Reading

Reading 2.2

Some people achieve iconic status. They are glorified after death, and their images appear on everything from T-shirts to coffee mugs. In the following text, *New York Times* columnist Larry Rohter examines the legacy of Che Guevara.

Che Today?

by Larry Rohter

1 Che Guevara is widely remembered today as a revolutionary figure; to some he's a heroic, Christ-like martyr, and to others he's the embodiment of a failed ideology. To still others,

Ernesto "Che" Guevara

he is just a commercialized emblem on a T-shirt. But for Latin Americans just now coming of age, yet another image of Che is starting to emerge: the romantic and tragic young adventurer who has as much in common with Jack Kerouac or James Dean as with Fidel Castro. The phenomenon began a decade ago with the publication of his long-suppressed memoir known in English as *The Motorcycle Diaries*, which has become a cult favourite among Latin American college students and young intellectuals.

2 Very few young people today would subscribe to Che's belief that power can be seized through guerrilla warfare. But they are disillusioned with the wholesale embrace of capitalism that occurred across the region during the 1990s. They see it as having aggravated economic and social inequities that he railed against, and they are looking for alternatives. Che provides that because he is "a figure who can constantly be examined and re-examined," as Jon Lee Anderson, author of *Che Guevara: A Revolutionary Life*, puts it. "To the younger, post-Cold-War generation of Latin Americans, Che stands up as the perennial Icarus, a self-immolating figure who represents the romantic tragedy of youth," he added. "Their Che is not just a potent figure of protest, but the idealistic, questioning kid who exists in every society and every time."

3 *The Motorcycle Diaries* retells the eight-month, 7,500-mile odyssey across five South American countries that Guevara, then an asthmatic twenty-three-year-old medical student, began in December 1951. Travelling first on a rickety motorcycle named "La Poderosa," the powerful one, and then as hitchhikers and stowaways, he and a friend crossed the pampas, traversed the Andes, and navigated the Amazon before arriving in Caracas, Venezuela, and going their separate ways.

4 Che was simply Ernesto Guevara then, and his account of the journey is a classic coming-of-age story: a voyage of adventure and self-discovery that is both political and personal. "We were just a pair of vagabonds with knapsacks on our backs, the dust of the road covering us, mere shadows of our old aristocratic egos," he writes when the pair reaches Valparaiso, Chile.

5 His companion on the trip, Alberto Granado Jiménez, is still alive and living in Cuba. At the age of eighty-two, he travelled recently to Brazil for the premiere of the film *The Motorcyle Diaries,* and he immediately noticed the change in Che's image. He said he found himself "surrounded by young people asking beautiful things, not just about the movie, but about what Ernesto and I were feeling back then," he said. "Practically nothing was asked about politics," Mr. Granado recalled, somewhat wistfully. "They were more interested in the human aspect, in the story of how two young men, two normal people but dreamers and idealists, set out on an adventure and, with optimism and impetuosity, achieve their objective."

6 The Cuban government, which regards itself as the custodian of Che's image and controls much of his literary estate, has never much liked *The Motorcycle Diaries*. The book remained unpublished until the early 1990s, and even today, the officially authorized *Complete Works of Ernesto Che Guevara* includes his famous essays, "On Guerrilla Warfare" and "Create Two, Three, Many Vietnams," but pointedly omits the diaries.

7 "The Cubans have excluded everything about Che that is not heroic, including that which is most deliciously human about him," said Mario O'Donnell, an Argentine psychoanalyst

and historian who is the author of a recent biography about Che. "The personal doubts, the sexual escapades, the moments when he and Granado are drunk, none of that fits with the immortal warrior they want to project."

8 That demystification is part of a broader process of de-Cubanizing Che. Though official Cuban accounts usually call him an "internationalist" (skipping any mention of his Argentine nationality), he spent only eight of his thirty-nine years in Cuba. In fact, he had renounced Cuban citizenship by the time of his death in 1967, when he was killed after the collapse of a guerrilla campaign in Bolivia.

9 Having grown up with Che as a brand name advertisement for protests of any sort, Latin Americans under forty may have trouble regarding him with the same reverence as their elders do. So while Che continues to be a universal point of reference, some recent artistic treatments of him have also been tinged with irony. In that vein, a Brazilian film comedy imagines that Che never died but escaped to the Amazon jungle where he runs a business selling T-shirts stamped with his own image. In Che's homeland, a popular singer-songwriter, Kevin Johansen, has a song called "McGuevara's or CheDonald's."

10 For an even younger generation, Che is perhaps becoming an even more remote figure who has already faded into history. "I never had a Che T-shirt or poster because ever since I was a kid, I saw him, like many people do, as a distant image," the twenty-five-year-old Mexican actor Gael García Bernal, who plays Che in the movie *The Motorcycle Diaries*, confessed to reporters at Cannes.

11 "That's what happens with icons," said José Rivera, a Puerto Rican playwright and screenwriter who wrote the screenplay for the movie. "They are recycled and made to wear the clothes of a new generation that is discovering them. We're not in the sixties anymore, so Che will not have the same power he had back then, and we will have to discover him in a new way."

Vocabulary and Comprehension

1 • Find a two-word expression in Paragraph 2 that means "complained about."

____

2 • In Paragraph 2, what is the meaning of *potent*? ______________________

3 • In which country was Che born? ______________________

4 • According to the essay, why did the Cuban government dislike *The Motorcycle Diaries*?

____

____

5 • In Paragraph 2, the author compares Che to Icarus. Icarus is a Greek god who attached wings with wax, and, defying his father, flew too close to the sun. The wax melted, his wings fell off, and he fell into the sea and died. How was Che like Icarus?

____

____

6 • In Paragraph 11, a Puerto Rican writer says that icons are "recycled and made to wear the clothes of a new generation that is discovering them." What does Che represent to youths today?

____

____

7 • What is the author's tone? You can choose more than one answer. Give an example from the text that shows the tone.

serious   cynical   sympathetic   nostalgic   sarcastic

Example: ____

Reading 2.3

In this excerpt from an essay by Alvaro Vargas Llosa, you will discover another side of the iconic figure, Che Guevara.

Che Guevara: The Killing Machine

by Alvaro Vargas Llosa

1 Che Guevara, who did so much (or was it so little?) to destroy capitalism, is now a quintessential capitalist brand. His likeness adorns mugs, baseball caps, bandanas, tank tops ... and of course those omnipresent T-shirts with the photograph taken by Alberto Korda of the socialist heartthrob in his beret during the early years of the revolution. Che happened to walk into the photographer's viewfinder—and into the image that, thirty-eight years after his death, is still the logo of revolutionary (or is it capitalist?) chic.

2 It is customary for followers of a cult not to know the real life story of their hero. (Many Rastafarians would renounce Haile Selassie if they had any notion of who he really was.) It is not surprising that Guevara's contemporary followers, his new post-communist admirers, also delude themselves by clinging to a myth.

3 Che Guevara might have been enamoured of his own death, but he was much more enamoured of other people's deaths. In April 1967, speaking from experience, he summed up his homicidal idea of justice in his "Message to the Tricontinental" essay: "hatred as an element of struggle, unbending hatred for the enemy, which pushes a human being beyond his natural limitations, making him into an effective, violent, selective, and cold-blooded killing machine."

4 In January 1957, as his diary from the Sierra Maestra indicates, Guevara shot Eutimio Guerra because he suspected him of passing on information: "I ended the problem with a .32-calibre pistol, in the right side of his brain ... His belongings were now mine." Later he shot Aristidio, a peasant who expressed the desire to leave whenever the rebels moved on. While he wondered whether this particular victim "was really guilty enough to deserve death," he had no qualms about ordering the death of Echevarría, a brother of one of his comrades, because of unspecified crimes: "He had to pay the price." At other times, he would simulate executions, without carrying them out, as a method of psychological torture.

5 Che's lust for power had other ways of expressing itself besides murder. In 1958, after taking the city of Sancti Spiritus, Guevara unsuccessfully tried to impose a kind of *shariah*, regulating relations between men and women, the use of alcohol, and informal gambling —a puritanism that did not exactly characterize his own way of life. He also ordered his

men to rob banks, a decision that he justified in a letter to Enrique Oltuski, a subordinate, in November of that year: "The struggling masses agree to robbing banks because none of them has a penny in them." This idea of revolution as a licence to reallocate property as he saw fit led the Marxist puritan to take over the mansion of an emigrant after the triumph of the revolution.

6 His stint as head of the National Bank, during which he printed bills signed "Che," has been summarized by his deputy, Ernesto Betancourt: "[He] was ignorant of the most elementary economic principles." Guevara's powers of perception regarding the world economy were famously expressed in 1961, at a hemispheric conference in Uruguay, where he predicted a 10 percent rate of growth for Cuba "without the slightest fear," and, by 1980, a per capita income greater than that of "the US today." In fact, by 1997, the thirtieth anniversary of his death, Cubans were dieting on a ration of five pounds of rice and one pound of beans per month, four ounces of meat twice a year, four ounces of soybean paste per week, and four eggs per month.

Vocabulary and Comprehension

1 • Find a word in Paragraph 1 that mean's "to decorate." ____________

2 • Find a word in Paragraph 4 that means "doubts; uneasy feelings."

____

3 • In the first two sentences of Paragraph 5, what is the author suggesting about Che Guevara?

a) Che was a hypocrite.

b) Che had strong spiritual beliefs.

c) Che was very puritanical.

4 • What are Vargas Llosa's four main complaints about Che Guevara?

____

____

____

____

5 • What is the author's tone? You can choose more than one answer. Give an example from the text that shows the tone.

serious cynical sympathetic nostalgic sarcastic

Example: ____________

Written Response

How does Larry Rohter's tone differ form Vargas Llosa's? In a paragraph, compare the two views of Che Guevara.

Listening •• Sports Heroes

Many sports fans are thrilled when their team wins and devastated when it loses. Why are athletes worshipped? Stephen Dubner, the author of *Confessions of a Hero-Worshipper*, discusses sports heroes.

Listening Comprehension

1 • What is *BIRGing*? ______________________________

2 • What happens to male fans when an athlete succeeds?

____

____

3 • What is *coffing*? ______________________________

4 • Who were the traditional heroes of the past?

____

____

5 • Why are athletes such glorious heroes?

____

____

____

6 • When there is a sports scandal, it is generally perceived as a larger tragedy than a political scandal. Why?

____

____

____

____

7 • How is hero-worship linked to religious worship or romantic love?

____

____

____

____

8 • Why is it artificial to think a living person will always remain heroic?

____

____

____

Speaking ·· An Influential Individual

You will do a presentation about a heroic or highly influential person. You will need to do some research on the Internet. Look for both positive and negative articles about that person. Your presentation will be more forceful and interesting if you can provide specific and detailed anecdotes.

You can choose a hero from any of the following categories:

sports   entertainment   politics   military   civilian

Structure

Your presentation should have the following format:

Introduction:	Give general background information about that hero. Why is he or she elevated and admired?
Body:	What are that hero's positive traits? Provide details and anecdotes.
	What are his or her negative traits? Provide details and anecdotes.
Conclusion:	Give your final view of the hero. Does it matter if the person has dark sides?

Presentation

- Don't read. You can use cue cards to guide yourself through the presentation.
- Use formal language.
- Practise and time yourself. Ensure that you speak for the time limit set by your teacher.
- Bring in visual support. For example, you can bring in a picture, T-shirt, or other item that has the hero's image.

Writing Topics

To review some of the vocabulary studied in this chapter, visit the companion website.

Write a composition about one of the following topics. Remember to include a thesis statement and provide supporting examples. Before handing in your work, refer to the Writing Checklist on the inside back cover.

1 • What is a hero? Write an essay defining heroes. Explain what three qualities make a person heroic.

2 • Which individual from the last century is most likely to be remembered and mythologized? Explain why.

3 • Why do people elevate and idolize others? What benefits do heroes give us?

4 • Who were our heroes in childhood? How do our idols change as we get older?

5 • Should Che Guevara be idolized? You can quote from Larry Rohter and Alvaro Vargas Llosa.

CHAPTER 3

•• We are each burdened with prejudice: against the poor or the rich, the smart or the slow, the gaunt or the obese. It is natural to develop prejudices. It is noble to rise above them. ••

Anonymous

Dealing with Differences

Is prejudice innate? Can we rise above it? In this chapter, you will explore the roots of racism and intolerance.

Warm Up •• Making Associations

The **Implicit Association Test** assumes that people make connections between familiar pairs of ideas. For example, if we hear the name "Robert," we automatically associate it with a man.

Try the following test. Be spontaneous. Don't spend too much time thinking about your choice. Just put a checkmark in either the right or left column.

Young person (under 25)		Old person (over 65)
☐	good decision-maker	☐
☐	active and healthy	☐
☐	patient	☐
☐	risk-taker	☐
☐	useful citizen	☐
☐	a burden on others	☐
☐	aggressive	☐
☐	sensual or sexy	☐
☐	wise	☐
☐	selfish	☐
☐	makes poor choices	☐
☐	bad driver	☐
☐	not attractive	☐

To develop your listening skills, visit the companion website.

Discussion

1 • What influences people to become prejudiced against other groups or cultures?

2 • Read the quotation at the beginning of this chapter. Do you agree that it is natural to develop prejudices?

•• The Implicit Association Test (IAT) was developed by Anthony G. Greenwald, Mahzarin Banaji, and Brian Nosek.

Reading

Reading Strategy

Recognizing Bias

There are several things you can do in order to critique a text.

1 • **Ask yourself who benefits.**

When you read, ask yourself who benefits from the publication of the text. If the story is about a political situation, ask yourself if the article favours one side over the other. If you read about a survey, determine who paid for the survey.

2 • **Examine the evidence.**

Ask yourself if the supporting evidence comes from a trustworthy source. Also read the examples critically to determine if they are relevant and reliable. For instance, is anecdotal evidence suggestive of a major trend or is it simply one particular reaction to a situation?

3 • **Determine if there is a bias.**

Remember that everyone has a bias. Our age, gender, racial, financial, and cultural background influence our opinions about issues. Nonetheless, newspaper and magazine writers try to appear objective when they write informative articles. When you read, ask yourself if the author is objective or subjective.

IN SUBJECTIVE WRITING, THE AUTHOR:	IN OBJECTIVE WRITING, THE AUTHOR:
• expresses a point of view and personal feelings (*I think …*) • makes statements that are one-sided (*Men are violent.*) • gives advice (*You can become addicted.*) • may ask rhetorical questions (*Why do we neglect the homeless?*) • uses emotionally loaded language (*She abandoned her son.*)	• does not express any feelings and appears neutral • describes facts without commenting on them • quotes the opinions of others instead of his or her own

Be careful. Sometimes writing that appears objective could be biased. For example, if an author disagrees with capital punishment, he or she could choose to interview people who also disagree with it. Thus, even though the author doesn't state an opinion, there is a bias. Therefore, as you read, you can ask yourself if the author is expressing his or her point of view. Try to recognize bias.

Reading Exercise

Look at the following excerpts, and then answer the questions that follow.

Sample 1

According to the National Highway Traffic Safety Administration, people over the age of sixty-five are three times more likely to be involved in a car crash than adults under sixty-five. Elderly motorists, who may suffer from failing eyesight, heart conditions, and mental incompetence, are killing themselves and others. They are crashing through blockades, driving off highways, going through stop signs and red lights, and generally causing havoc on roadways. Why are the driver's licences of elderly residents automatically renewed each year? As soon as people reach sixty-five, they should be forced to undergo driving tests on a yearly basis. The tests should ensure that the driver is mentally and physically competent. Then and only then can we reduce the slaughter on our highways.

From "Deadly Drivers" by Graham Anders

1 • Is this text an example of objective or subjective writing? ______________
Highlight a sentence from the text as proof of your choice.

2 • What is the author's main point? ______________________________

____

3 • Is the author biased, and if so, how? ___________________________

____

Sample 2

Beatriz Luna and her colleagues from the University of Pittsburgh used a type of MRI that enables researchers to observe the brain as it is functioning. Luna gave teens and adults a task that required them to control an impulse. She found that both teens and adults did equally well at the task, but that they used different parts of their brains to perform it. The adults relied largely on brain areas involved in automatic responses. The teens, however, relied largely on a frontal-lobe area involved in intense thinking activities, such as calculating and reasoning. The result suggests that teens have to concentrate very hard to control their impulses—much harder than adults do. As a result, teens could have more difficulty stopping themselves from committing crimes, says Luna. Such evidence could suggest to the courts that a teen's criminal actions may not be totally voluntary, she adds.

From "The Adolescent Brain" by Ingrid Wickelgren

1 • Is this text an example of objective or subjective writing? ______________

2 • What main point is the author probably trying to make? ____________

____

3 • Is the author biased, and if so, how? ___________________________

____

____

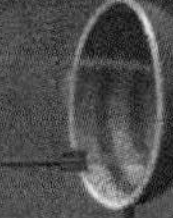

Pair Reading Activity (Optional)

Find a partner. One of you can read "Racism's Source," and the other can read "P is for Prejudice." Answer the questions that follow your reading. Later you will share your information with your partner.

Reading 3.1

Gwynne Dyer is a native of Newfoundland, Canada. He is currently a London-based independent journalist whose articles are published in forty-five countries. In the following essay, Dyer examines the roots of racism.

Racism's Source

by Gwynne Dyer

1 "What are you doing here in Germany?" asked the three drunken youths when they ran into Alberto Adriano in Dessau one Saturday night in June. "I live here," Adriano might have replied, but he didn't get the chance. Enrico Hilprecht, twenty-four, and Frank Miethbauer and Christian Richter, both sixteen, were still rhythmically kicking and stamping on his head with their steel-capped boots and chanting "Get out of our country, you n—— pig" when the police pulled up and arrested them.

2 Adriano's skinhead killers went on trial with Germany's chief federal prosecutor, Kay Nehm, personally leading the prosecution. Hilprecht was sent to prison for life, and the two teenagers were each given nine-year sentences.

3 Germany is considering a ban on the neo-Nazi National Party of Germany, whose members are involved in a high proportion of attacks on racial minorities.

4 These responses would be more reassuring, however, if the xenophobia were confined to a few neo-fascists. It isn't; it's a popular sport throughout eastern Germany.

5 So is there some special wickedness in Germans that makes them instinctive racists, in Hitler's time or in our own? One doubts that Christian Richardson would think so. Richardson is English, and moved to Dublin last year to be with his twenty-four-year-old Irish girlfriend. He quickly found a good job in the booming Irish capital, and last June his parents came over from England to visit him. His father is white and his mother is black, which would not have turned any heads in his native city of Bristol. In Dublin, it nearly got them killed.

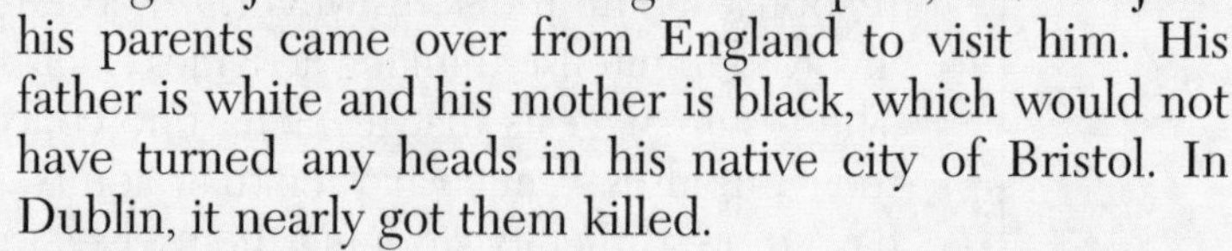

6 Walking back from a restaurant right in the centre of Dublin, the three were set upon by white Irish youths. Christian Richardson's father was stabbed six times in the neck and back as he tried to protect his Jamaican-born wife. He almost died.

7 His son treated it as an isolated incident and stayed in Dublin—until it happened again in mid-August as he was bicycling to work. "It was broad daylight," said Richardson. "Three lads shouted a load of racist abuse at me as I passed them, and then started coming after me. I was terrified. I thought, 'That's it. I'm off. No way I'm staying around to take this.' I just packed my bag and got on a plane."

8 There is racist violence in England, too, but Richardson clearly feels a lot safer in England than in Ireland. As for eastern Germany, it is off the scale: racial attacks there are four times more frequent than in Britain. So what did East Germany and Ireland have in common that could account for their brutal racism? Not much, on the face of it.

9 Ireland is Catholic; eastern Germany is Protestant. Ireland was a British colony; eastern Germany (as Prussia) was a great power. Germany is one of the poorest regions of the European Union with unemployment of more than 17 percent; Ireland is now the "Celtic Tiger" with an economy growing three times faster than the European average and only 4 percent unemployment.

10 But there is one common factor. These are both places where almost everybody was white until recently. Perhaps the problem is not innate, ineradicable racism, but just the panicky reaction of an isolated population when its ethnic homogeneity and cultural conformity begins to be challenged.

11 German politicians (and now some Irish ones too) respond to outbreaks of racial violence with demands for tighter immigration controls, as if the problem were too many foreigners. But there is a strong case for saying that the real problem is too few.

12 Compare Britain, which has had large-scale immigration for over a generation and is now a fairly relaxed multi-racial society, to Ireland, a society only recently emerged from the Catholic nationalist dream of a single people united by religion, language, and history. Or compare former West Germany, which has taken in lots of immigrants since the 1960s, to former Communist East Germany, which spent forty years living in a cave.

13 The lowest rate of racist violence in Germany is in the state of Saarland, on the French border, where 8.2 percent of the population is foreign-born. The highest rate is in Saxony-Anhalt, where only 1.7 percent are foreigners, and an even tinier proportion are non-white. All the other eastern states share the same pattern of high anti-foreign violence and practically no foreigners.

14 So maybe the real solution is to flood the place with people from elsewhere, and wait for the locals to get used to diversity. Of course, first you have to figure out some way to persuade the outsiders to stay.

Comprehension

1 • How do Ireland and eastern Germany compare? Fill in the following chart.

	IRELAND	EASTERN GERMANY
Religion		
Wealth and economy		
Unemployment rate		
General race of population until recently		

Indicate if the following statements are true or false. If the statement is false, write down the true information.

2 • Alberto Adriano said "I live here" to his attackers. .... T F

---

3 • England is more multi-ethnic than Ireland. .... T F

---

4 • Poverty and unemployment are the main factors in racist attacks....... T F

---

5 • The author, Gwynne Dyer, does not believe that there is a "special wickedness" in Germans. .... T F

Critical Thinking

6 • What introduction style does the author use?

a) contrasting information **b)** general background **c)** anecdote

7 • Is the text objective or subjective? Explain your answer.

---

8 • What is the author's central argument? How can we get rid of racism?

Reading 3.2

Toronto-based Allen Abel is an author, television personality, and documentary producer. In the following essay, Abel examines the work of McGill University professor Dr. Frances Aboud.

P Is for Prejudice

by Allen Abel

1 A five-year-old girl we'll call Danielle crosses the hallway from her kindergarten class to a tiny meeting room at a public school in central Montreal. Waiting for her are McGill University professor of psychology Frances Aboud and one of her graduate students.

2 Dr. Aboud has brought a binder of pictures for Danielle to consider. The illustrations are simple drawings of boys and girls, men and women, two to each page, each pair identical except for the colour of their skin and the texture of their hair. Each page is linked to a question, which the graduate student reads to the little girl.

3 "Some boys are mean. When they come home from school, and their dog comes to meet them, they kick their dog. Who is mean?" Danielle points to the brown-skinned boy. The testing goes on: "Some boys are clean ... Some girls are not good-looking ... Some boys are kind ... Some boys are nice ... Some girls won't let others play ... Some men don't share. Who won't share?" Five times out of six, Danielle, who is white, selects the white character for a positive attribute. And five times out of six, she chooses the black subject as the negative.

4 It is easy to suspect that she answers in this way because her parents have sown the seeds of hate within her, or because she is living in a racist world. Perhaps her teacher has failed, or television has tainted her mind. But Dr. Aboud believes that little Danielle is prejudiced because she is developing normally and because she is five years old. Discrimination was wired into her brain at conception—as it is into my brain, and yours. "Prejudice is biological," the professor says. It is a powerful statement on which she has staked her academic reputation.

5 At McGill since 1975, Dr. Aboud has specialized in childhood racial awareness, testing thousands of children as young as three with picture books and flash cards to calibrate—and perhaps one day to cure—the impulse that may be inborn. "Any parent knows that when you walk down the street with a two-year-old, they comment on the colour of people," she says. "'There's a pink lady; there's a brown lady.' At that age, they just see colour."

6 "At about the age of four or five, they begin to realize that skin colour is a constancy and it's attached to them. It kicks in that they are part of a group, and they prefer people whom they can identify as part of their group. Many things are important clues in figuring out who belongs to which group, but skin colour and hair texture are the two big ones. This is where prejudice comes in."

7 Dr. Aboud says that at five years of age, about 50 to 60 percent of children have negative "out-group" feelings, which is to say that they distrust anyone outside their own group. "It's not that they don't like the other groups, but they prefer their own," she says. "It's not hatred of the others—it's suspicion of differences."

8 At age four or five, Dr. Aboud notes, children do not have the verbal skills to express their racial attitudes, and parents who are careful not to discuss racial issues in the home are often shocked to learn that their kids have registered as prejudiced on her "Who is mean?" tests. "I tell the parents, 'It doesn't come from you.' So they blame the school—they think it has to come from *somewhere.* I tell them it doesn't come from school, either. So they think we cause it by doing our tests."

9 Nearly everything in our political and popular culture argues that Frances Aboud must be wrong. The French novelist and poet Tahar Ben Jelloun affirms it in *Racism Explained to My Daughter*: "No one is born racist. If your parents or the people around you don't put racist ideas into your head, there's no reason you should become so."

10 Psychologist William Bukowski at Concordia University is convinced that Frances Aboud is getting it right. "What she has shown is that children of a certain age are *all* prejudiced, regardless of what views their parents have," Dr. Bukowski tells me. "Prejudice gives you a very simple way of seeing the world. Life is complex—and when you're a child, you've just begun to see that complexity. The desire for simplicity is a human frailty, and that is translated in a child's mind into a preference for in-group members."

11 If little Danielle continues along the normal path of human cognitive development, her preference for people with her skin colour and hair type over "different" people will intensify until she is seven, then diminish measurably.

12 "Eight is the age of reason," says Frances Aboud. "They come out of their egocentric state and realize that there are other perspectives: whites can be both positive and negative; blacks can be both positive and negative. The same kids, when we test them at five, they're prejudiced, and when we test them again at nine, they're not."

13 "The question is, why do some kids remain prejudiced?" says Professor Anna Beth Doyle of Concordia, Dr. Aboud's long-time collaborator. "What we need to find out next is what happens to some kids that they *don't* continue to [be racist], and to some kids that they *do*."

14 Twenty-five years of research have taught Dr. Frances Aboud what works in building tolerance, and what doesn't. What does not work, she says, is the nominal mixing of the tribes. "It's not just integrating the schools, where you put them together," she says. "You have to have them in the same class, intensively working on projects in mixed pairs or in mixed groups. Having a succession of cross-race friends—friends you respect and trust—has a positive impact later on. But it's got to be more than one [friend], and it's got to be at the level of real co-operative learning and working together."

15 "Prejudice *can* be changed," she says, "but you've got to overdo it—you've got to be explicit about it. You have to talk specifically about bias and how to intervene to stop it."

Comprehension

1 • What are Dr. Aboud's conclusions regarding the stages of development and prejudice?

	RACIST TENDENCIES, ATTITUDES, BELIEFS
Age 2	
Age 4–5	
Age 8–9	

Indicate if the following statements are true or false according to the text. If the statement is false, write down the true information.

2 • Parents and a racist society are to blame when children are racist...... T F

____

3 • Children pass through a stage where they have prejudice tendencies..... T F

____

4 • About 50 to 60 percent of five-year-olds hate people from other racial groups. . . . . T F

____

5 • If children go to mixed-race schools, they will lose their racist tendencies. . . . . T F

____

6 • What is the point of Dr. Aboud's research?

____

____

Critical Thinking

7 • Is the text objective or subjective? Explain your answer.

____

____

8 • In which paragraph does the author express an opposing viewpoint. _______

9 • According to Dr. Aboud, how can we build a less racist society?

____

____

Pair Reading: Share Your Information

Compare "Racism's Source" and "P is for Prejudice." Sit with someone who has read the other text and share information.

1 • What causes prejudice?

GWYNNE DYER	DR. ABOUD

2 • How do Dyer and Aboud prove their points?

GWYNNE DYER	DR. ABOUD

3 • What is Dyer's or Aboud's opinion about how to build a less prejudiced society?

GWYNNE DYER	DR. ABOUD

To work on your writing skills, visit the companion website.

Discussion or Written Response

1 • How do Dyer and Aboud contradict each other? How are their ideas similar?

2 • Which argument makes more sense? Why?

Tip Grammar

Say vs. *Tell*

Use *say* in direct and indirect quotations. In direct quotations, follow *say* with the actual words that were said.

Aboud **says**, "Eight is the age of reason."

Bukowski **said** that he agreed with Aboud.

You *tell* something to somebody. *Tell* is followed by a noun or pronoun.

Aboud **told** the journalist about her experiment.

Also use *tell* in such expressions as *tell a lie*, *tell the truth*, and *tell a secret*.

You can practise using these terms in *Open Road English Grammar*, Unit 12.

Speaking •• Present an Important Issue

Think about a controversial issue in your community. Find an issue that has directly affected you or someone you know. For example, if you know someone who dropped out of high school, suggest ways that the high school system could be improved. If you know someone who has had a drug addiction, explain how governments or family can help deal with that problem.

Possible topics: body image, drug use, dropout rates, drinking and driving, ways to improve colleges, smoking laws, daycare, gambling, environmental problems, cost of student housing, your choice

Structure

You can do some research. Your presentation should have the following structure.

- **Introduction:** Begin with an anecdote, general background information, or historical background information. End with your **thesis statement**. In other words, state your point of view about the problem.

- **Prove there is a problem:** Explain *why* it is a problem that we should think about. Include an anecdote about you or someone you know.
- **Explain how to solve the problem:** Suggest at least two actions that individuals, schools, governments, or others can do to solve the problem or to improve the situation.
- **Make a final concluding statement.**

Preparation

- Prepare! Time yourself. Your presentation must be at least four minutes long.
- Do not read. Use cue cards with key words.

Listening •• Pakistan

Calgary freelance journalist Aziza Sindhu travelled to her parents' home in Pakistan to explore her culture and heritage. She discovered much more than she bargained for. Listen to the interview with Aziza and answer the questions that follow.

Listening Comprehension

1 • Give background information on Aziza Sindhu.

a) How old is she? ______________________

b) Before visiting her half-brother, when did Aziza last visit Pakistan?

____

c) How did she feel about her Pakistani roots growing up in Calgary?

____

2 • In Pakistan, Aziza's half-brother, Seemab, became her tour guide. Aziza tells Seemab about her lifestyle in Canada. Describe her lifestyle.

____

____

3 • What is Seemab's opinion of Aziza's lifestyle in Canada?

____

____

4 • How did Aziza escape her parents' desire to set her up in an arranged marriage?

____

____

5 • Why does Aziza think that Seemab is a hypocrite? What does she discover?

____

____

To practise your speaking skills, visit the companion website.

6 • What advice does Aziza give Seemab about his marriage? ____________

____

7 • What secret does Aziza discover about her father? ____________

____

8 • What "price" did Seemab pay in order to keep his natural father in his life?

____

____

9 • What do Aziza and Seemab discover that they have in common?

____

____

Reading

Reading 3.3

Drew Hayden Taylor, Ojibwa playwright and novelist, discusses common misconceptions about Canadian natives in the following essay. Before you read, look at the photo. What impressions do the tourist shop souvenirs give of Canadian natives?

Seeing Red over Myths
by Drew Hayden Taylor

1 A year and a half ago, my Mohawk girlfriend and I (a fellow of proud Ojibwa heritage) found ourselves in the history-rich halls of Europe, lecturing on native issues, the propaganda and the reality, at a university deep in the heart of northeastern Germany. Then one young lady, a student at this former communist university, put up her hand and asked an oddly naive question, something like, "Do Indian women shave their legs and armpits like other North American women?" This was not the strangest question I've had put to me. I keep a list, which includes, "I'm phoning from Edinburgh, Scotland, and am doing research on natives in the 1930s. Can you send information?" or "Where can I get my hands on some Inuit throat singers?"

2 But unbeknownst to me, the shaving of extremities in Europe is a largely unexplored area of female hygiene; evidently this topic warranted investigation as to its possible Aboriginal origin. But the question presented a rather obvious example of the issue that permeates North America: the myth of pan-Indianism. The young lady had begun her question with "Do Indian women ...?" Sometimes the questioner substitutes First Nations/native/Aboriginal/indigenous for Indian. However it's worded, it reveals a persistent belief that we are all one people.

3 Within the borders of what is now referred to as Canada, there are more than fifty distinct and separate languages and dialects. And each distinct and separate language and dialect has emerged from a distinct and separate culture. I tried to tell this woman that her question couldn't be answered because, technically, there is no "Indian/First Nations/Aboriginal." To us, there is only the Cree, the Ojibwa, the Salish, the Innu, the Shuswap, and so on.

4 I find myself explaining this point with annoying frequency, not just in Europe, but here in Canada, at the Second Cup, Chapters, or the bus station. The power of that single myth is incredible. When people ask me, "What do First Nations people want?" how do I answer? Some of the Mi'kmaq want to catch lobster; some of the Cree want to stop the flooding and logging of their territory in northern Manitoba, Alberta, and Quebec; the Mohawk want the right to promote their own language, and I know bingo is in there somewhere.

5 That's why every time I see a TV news report talking about the plight of the Aboriginal people, I find myself screaming "Which People? Be specific!" That's why I never watch television in public.

6 Such is the power of myths. By their very definition, they're inaccurate or incomplete. Now you know why we as native people (see, I do it myself) prefer not to use the term "myth" when referring to the stories of our ancestors, as in "The Myths and Legends of Our People." There is something inherently wrong about starting a traditional story with "This is one of the myths that was passed down from our grandfathers ..." Literally translated, it means, "This is a lie that was handed down by our grandfathers ..."

7 The preferred term these days is *teachings*—as in, "Our teachings say ..." It's certainly more accurate, because it recognizes the fact that most teachings exist for a purpose—that there's some nugget of metaphor or message within the subtext. And in the native (there I go again!) way, we like to accentuate the positive. (Important note: The word *legend* can also be used instead of *teachings*, provided you have oral permission from a recognized elder, or written permission from an Aboriginal academic—any Nation will do).

8 The myth of pan-Indianism is not the only one rooted in the Canadian psyche. A good percentage of Canadians believe that there's a strong Aboriginal tradition of alcoholism. In Kenora, a decade or so ago, someone told me that in one month alone there had been almost three hundred arrests of Aboriginals for alcohol-related offences. And Kenora's not that big a town. The statistic frightened me—until it was explained that rather than confirming the mind-boggling image of three hundred drunken Indians running through the Kenora streets, it signified the same dozen people who just got arrested over and over and over again. It's all in how you read the statistic. And nobody told me how many white people had been arrested over and over again. It's all in how you read that statistic.

9 While acknowledging that certain communities do, indeed, suffer from substance-abuse problems (like many non-native communities, I might add), I can safely say that neither myself, my girlfriend, my mother, my best friend, nor most of the other people of Aboriginal descent I consider friends and acquaintances are alcoholics. Which makes me wonder why this myth is so persuasive.

10 It's also believed by a good percentage of Canadians that all native people are poor. Unfortunately, many communities do suffer from mind-numbing poverty, as do many non-native communities. But contrary to popular belief, capitalism was not a foreign

concept to Canada's earliest inhabitants. There were levels of wealth and status back then; today, instead of counting their horses, the rich might count their horsepower.

11 Several weeks ago, a Toronto newspaper attacked a rumour about a coalition of Aboriginal people who had expressed interest in buying the **Ottawa Senators**. The columnist thought the idea preposterous: "These are the same people who can't afford to pay tax on a pack of smokes; the same people who are so poor they claim government policy is forcing them to live in neighbourhoods where a rusted car with more than one flat tire is considered a lawn ornament." Well, the ratio of rusted-car-on-lawn to no-rusted-car-on-lawn is so disproportionate, it's hardly worth mentioning.

12 Yes, there are some wealthy native people out there (I wish I knew more of them personally). But their existence is a hard idea to accept when the media only feature First Nations stories on the desperate and the tragic.

13 So where does this leave us? I was asked to write an essay on the "myths of a common Indian identity," which, as I translate it, means that I was asked to comment on lies about something that doesn't exist. That sounds more like politics to me. But if you're still curious about whether Indian women shave their legs and armpits, you'll have to ask one. I'm not telling.

•• **Ottawa Senators** A professional hockey team in Ottawa

Vocabulary

1 • Write the letter of the correct definition in the space provided. The paragraph number is in parentheses.

TERM		DEFINITION
1. permeates (2)	______	a. small piece
2. plight (5)	______	b. absurd and ridiculous
3. nugget (7)	______	c. difficult situation
4. preposterous (11)	______	d. spreads through an area

Comprehension

2 • What are some alternative terms for *native*? ____________________________

____

3 • How does the author introduce his essay?

a) historical information **b)** contrasting position **c)** anecdote

4 • According to Hayden Taylor, what are some incorrect beliefs that people have about natives?

____

____

____

5• Hayden Taylor refutes common misconceptions with factual, anecdotal, and statistical support. Give an example of each one.

Fact: ____________________

Anecdote: ____________________

Statistic: ____________________

6• What is the difference between a *teaching* and a *myth*? ____________________

____

7• Human beings tend to make broad generalizations about most categories of people. What are some generalizations about Canadians, Americans, and Mexicans?

Canadians: ____________________

Americans: ____________________

Mexicans: ____________________

8• Why do people make generalizations about other cultures or groups?

____

____

____

Writing Topics

To review some of the vocabulary studied in this chapter, visit the companion website.

Write a composition about one of the following topics. Remember to include a thesis statement and provide supporting examples. Before handing in your work, refer to the Writing Checklist on the inside back cover.

1• "If history teaches anything, it's that there is no such thing as a pure culture. All cultures are the product of earlier cultures mixing, changing each other, and producing something new." (John Bemrose, "Rails of Reconciliation," *Maclean's*)

If you disagree with Bemrose's statement, explain how your family or cultural group has a pure, distinct culture. Mention three things that differentiate your family's culture from that of other societies.

If you agree with Bemrose's statement, explain how cultures are currently overlapping in your society. Mention how your community's culture has been influenced by other cultures around you.

2• Compare and contrast Gwynne Dyer's views about prejudice with those expressed by Dr. Aboud. How are they similar? How are they different?

3• What are some problems with nationalism? Think of some ways that nationalism can be harmful or helpful.

4• Drew Hayden Taylor writes about the myth of pan-Indianism. What myths or stereotypes exist about your culture, gender, or age group? Compare the myths with the reality.

CHAPTER 4

The Age of Persuasion

•• For manipulation to be most effective, evidence of its presence should be nonexistent. ••

Herbert Schiller

Every time you read a newspaper, drive past a billboard, search on the Internet, or watch a television program, you are exposed to advertising and persuasive techniques. In this chapter, you will read about our age of persuasion and the ease with which members of the public can be manipulated.

Warm Up •• Childhood and the Media

Work with a partner to complete the following tasks.

- Discuss how to complete each of the questions, filling the blanks with *do*, *does*, *did*, *is*, *am*, *are*, *was*, *were*, *have*, or *has*.
- Ask your partner the questions and write his or her answers in the space provided.

Partner's name: ______________________

1 • What ___were___ your favourite television programs when you were a child? List at least three programs.

I Don't remember the names

2 • About how many hours per day ___did___ you watch TV when you were a child?

3 hours

3 • ___Did___ your parents restrict your television viewing in any way during your childhood? Explain.

3 hours maximum then go play outside

4 • What ___was___ the most popular "girl" toys during your childhood?

Barbies

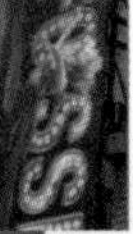

5 • What ___was___ the most popular "boy" toys during your childhood?

Lego

6 • As a child, what toys ___did___ you want because they were widely advertised?

Electronic games

7 • These days, what brands of clothing products ___are___ considered "cool" for your generation?

Anything

8 • ___Have___ you ever regretted buying or receiving a product (cereal, toys, clothing, shoes, and so on) just because it was very effectively marketed? Give at least two examples.

No

9 • Think back over your life. What marketing campaigns ___have___ been particularly successful? Give at least two examples. You might think of items you have bought because of the brand name.

Nike « Just do it »

Discussion

1 • What are some common features of toys marketed to girls? Think about the colours, functions, and types of toys. Also think about the activities that the toys encourage.

2 • What are some common features of toys marketed to boys? Think about the colours, functions, and types of toys. Also think about the activities that the toys encourage.

3 • What toys are gender-neutral?

4 • Some consumer groups believe that all advertising to children—for example, during Saturday morning cartoons—should be banned. What do you think?

To develop your listening skills, visit the companion website.

Written Response

Write a paragraph about your partner's reponses.

Tip Grammar

Possessive Forms

When more than one person possesses something, ensure that you place the apostrophe in the correct position. If the plural noun is regular, place the apostrophe after the final *s* to form the possessive.

the toys of the girls	the girls**'** toys

If the plural noun is irregular, add -*'s* to form the possessive.

the program of the children	the children**'s** program

Reading

Reading Strategy

Determining the Audience and Purpose

The audience is the intended reader. Writers often change the tone and vocabulary to suit the specific audience of males, females, executives, employees, children, and so on. When you read, ask yourself who the audience is.

Also ask yourself what the author's main purpose is. The purpose could be one or more of the following.

1 • to entertain	• The author hopes to get an emotional response from the reader. The text may evoke laughter, tears, anger, frustration, or shock.
2 • to inspire	• The author hopes to encourage and motivate the reader.
3 • to persuade	• The author expresses an opinion and hopes to influence the reader.
4 • to inform	• The author presents information about a topic. The author tries to remain neutral and does not intend to persuade the reader.

Reading 4.1

In the following essay, Dorothy Nixon looks at the world of gender and toys.

Put GI Barbie in the Bargain Bin

by Dorothy Nixon

1 It may not be the fashionable or politically correct thing to say, but boys gravitate toward violent action toys and girls toward pretty, passive toys. For example, boys like trucks, baseballs, and guns; girls prefer baby dolls, Barbie dolls, and glittery fake jewelry. Few people, old, young, married, or single, would have any trouble at all adding to this list. If

we asked these people why boys want action toys and girls want passive toys, a nature-versus-nurture debate would likely break out. One camp (nurture) argues that children are conditioned by society to choose certain toys; another camp (nature) claims that girls and boys have an inborn toy preference.

2 "Nurture" people say toys are agents of socialization. Once upon a time, children's toys were merely miniature versions of adult tools: sewing sets for girls and play hammers for boys. Because childhood was short, the children soon graduated to the real thing. So, if boys liked to play with guns, and girls preferred to play with dolls, it is because they wanted their parents' approval, and they hoped to be prepared for their adult roles.

3 "Nature" people believe toy preference is encoded in our genes. They could point us toward modern scientific research. A study finds that boys' brains are wired to hit the target, even if most males today do not hunt, hence the male sex's attraction to guns, basketball, and video games. Another study shows that girls exposed to too much testosterone in the womb tend to have very "masculine" tastes in toys (trucks and Meccano sets) even if their mothers are domestic goddesses. So, if boys like to play with guns, it is because men *throughout the ages* have been hunters and warriors. If girls like to play with dolls and decorate themselves, it is because women *throughout the ages* have raised children and decorated themselves.

4 Today the debate gets even stickier: Modern girls may be "liberated," believing the world is their oyster and that no future career is off limits, even that of an astronaut. But ask any female doctor or stockbroker and she is just as likely to tell you that her favourite childhood toy was her Easy-Bake Oven or My Little Pony. Why is this? Well, score one for the nurture side: These future career girls must have been persuaded by all the gender-biased advertising they watched. Or maybe "pretend cooking" improves math skills and "pretend grooming" prepares a person to be a more caring doctor.

5 It is a circular debate, a veritable chicken-and-egg situation, and one that leaves the toy industry unfazed. Companies spend gazillions on market research and advertising, and generally stack the toy store shelves with traditional fare for one reason: because it sells—violent, action-oriented toys for boys, and pretty, passive toys for girls.

6 Every once in a while, the marketing wizards pay lip service to today's expanding career options for women and give us a Scientist Barbie complete with a tiny chemistry set as an accessory. But heaven forbid should little Johnnie plead for his parents to buy him that Scientist Barbie. After all, it is acceptable for girls to foray, occasionally, into the world of boy-style play (what are tomboys, after all?), but for boys the opposite "sissified" behaviour is taboo. Why is this? One child development expert, D. R. Shaffer, suggests a possible answer: "The major task for young girls is to learn how not to be babies, whereas young boys must learn how not to be girls."

Looking at Language

1 • Paragraph 6 ends with a quotation. Why is there a colon (:) instead of a comma (,) directly before the quotation?

____

____

Is the final period before or after the quotation marks? __________

Vocabulary and Comprehension

2 • Define *fare* as it is used in Paragraph 5. ~~toys~~ material products

3 • Find a three-word expression in Paragraph 6 that means "pretend to support something."

Pay lip service

4 • Find a word in Paragraph 6 that means "to venture or enter something new."

~~extending~~ foray

5 • What main question is Nixon trying to answer? ~~Who's right~~ Why girls/boys play with
~~Nurture or Nature~~

6 • What is Nixon suggesting in the title of this essay? Don't try to make boys toys for girls

7 • Using your own words, sum up the main "nature" versus "nurture" arguments.

Nature: Inside them (when born)

____

____

Nurture: Learned

____

____

8 • Who is the audience for this essay? **a)** adults **b)** children

Explain your answer. sophisticated language

9 • What is Nixon's answer to her central question? __________

____

Discussion

1 • In the conclusion, Nixon suggests that girls can cross gender boundaries more easily than boys. Why is this?

2 • In the past, toys were organized according to gender. Do most toy stores still do that? Why?

Listening ·· The Age of Persuasion

Terry O'Reilly examines marketing and manipulation in this excerpt from his program, "The Age of Persuasion."

Listening Comprehension

1 • What ingredients went into Hub Beardsley's invention?

____

2 • What inspiring idea did the marketing team have when they created the Alka Seltzer ad?

____

____

3 • How did the new advertising method help sales? _______________

____

____

To practise your reading skills, visit the companion website.

4 • What three-word directions on shampoo bottles help increase consumption?

____

5 • Complete this marketing truism: _______________ of your business comes from _______________ of your customers.

6 • Who were the Kaiser Foil advertisements aimed at? _______________

____

7 • How were the Kaiser Foil ads effective? _______________

____

____

____

8 • What is the main point of this listening segment? _______________

____

____

Speaking ·· Fact or Fantasy

Survey some classmates. Get into a team of about five students to answer the following questions.

1 • Are the following statements true or false? In the space provided, indicate how many of you think the statement is a fact and how many think it is fantasy.

	FACT	FANTASY
a) It is possible to create a society where everybody has equal wealth.		
b) Reincarnation is true: we have all had past lives.		
c) Every person has the potential to be evil.		
d) Some psychics and mediums can contact the dead.		
e) Heinz really makes the best ketchup.		
f) The universe is expanding.		
g) People have mysteriously disappeared in the Bermuda Triangle.		
h) Capital punishment helps to lower the crime rate.		
i) Horoscopes provide useful information about future events.		
j) Global warming is serious and threatens life on earth.		
k) Human beings have walked on the moon.		
l) If all children were deeply loved, none would become criminals.		
m) Brand-name breakfast cereals are better than generic cereals.		
n) People are safer when they have guns in their homes.		
o) Some people can see the future.		
p) Products that are more expensive than their competitors also have higher quality.		
q) Generally, women do not make good leaders, and that is why there are so few female leaders.		
r) Aliens have visited the earth.		

Discussion

With a group of students, discuss the following questions.

2 • Are any items on the list definitely factual? Which ones?

3 • Are any items definitely fantasies? Which ones?

4 • Explain why you think some sentences are factual and others aren't. What criteria are you using to judge them?

Reading Strategy

Identify Cognates

Cognates, also known as word twins, are words that may look and sound alike in many languages and have the same meaning. For example, the English word *responsible* has the same meaning as the French or Spanish word *responsable*, although the words are spelled differently.

Sometimes words in different languages look alike but do not have the same meanings. Such words are called false cognates. For example, in English, *fabric* means "cloth," whereas in French, *fabriquer* means "to create." If you are not sure of a word's meaning, consult a dictionary.

If you come across an English word that looks similar to a word in your own language, check how the word is being used in context. It may or may not mean the same thing in English as in your language.

Reading 4.2

Advertisers aren't the only ones who effectively manipulate the public. Orson Welles was an artist, actor, playwright, director, producer, and radio star. When he was just twenty-one, he founded the Mercury Theatre and performed in radio plays and Broadway shows. When he presented the radio drama *The War of the Worlds*, he was accused of manipulating the public.

As you read the following text, keep in mind that in those days, radio was a relatively new and powerful medium and television was not yet a fixture in people's homes.

The Night the Martians Attacked

by Lee Krystek

1 Sunday, October 30, 1938, was "mischief night," and it was quiet in greater New York City. Thirty-two million people sat down by their radios to tune in and catch their favourite shows. *Charlie McCarthy* was on at 8 o'clock. About ten minutes into the program a "less than compelling" singer took the microphone, which resulted in a number of listeners changing the dial, mid-show. At WABC, in New York, they found what was apparently a program of dance music: Ramon Raquello and his orchestra from the Meridian Room of the Park Plaza Hotel.

2 Suddenly the broadcast was interrupted by a series of news bulletins. A large meteor had impacted in New Jersey near Grover's Mill. The object turned out not to be a meteor, but a metal cylinder. The cylinder opened and Martians, driving huge fighting machines, emerged. They were advancing upon New York City.

3 Within thirty minutes, the voice of a radio reporter—supposedly covering the event from a window in Manhattan—told of a gas attack on the city: "Smoke comes out ... black smoke, drifting over the city. People in the streets see it now. They're running toward the East River ... thousands of them, dropping like rats. Now the smoke's spreading faster. It's reached Times Square. People are trying to run away from it, but it's no use. They're falling like flies. Now the smoke's crossing Sixth Avenue ... Fifth Avenue ... one hundred yards away ... it's fifty feet ..."

4 Then the reporter stopped talking. There was silence for a few seconds. Then listeners heard the plaintive cry of a ham radio operator: "Isn't there anyone on the air? Isn't there anyone?"

5 Throughout New York, people panicked. They ran out in the streets ready to evacuate the city. Others called relatives on the telephone to warn them. Some called the police. A few simply broke down in tears. Apparently not many of them listened to what came next on the radio: An announcement that they had been listening to a *Mercury Theatre on the Air* production of H. G. Wells's *War of the Worlds*.

6 Many years after the event, Orson Welles, the producer of the Mercury Theatre, claimed he had "merrily anticipated" the kind of response the program drew.

7 *The Mercury Theatre on the Air*, like most radio shows in those days, was done live. It was also broadcast across the United States on the Columbia Broadcasting System. The program started with an opening narration by Orson Welles himself, and then switched to the dance music that was then interrupted by the bulletins. By the time the script had reached the point of black smoke obliterating the city, the cast knew something was up. The CBS switchboard was jammed with calls.

8 The next day, the newspapers reported that thousands of people called the police, newspapers, and radio stations throughout cities in the United States and Canada. Evening worship services in some churches were interrupted by the news, and a few turned into "end of the world" prayer meetings. At St. Michael's Hospital in Newark, fifteen people were treated for shock and hysteria, a scene repeated throughout New York area medical facilities. Some people claimed that the radio show had nearly given them a heart attack.

9 Because the broadcast had been carried throughout the country, the effect was nationwide. Listeners in the western United States, though not fearing immediate danger for themselves, called relatives and friends back east who had not heard the program. This further fuelled the panic.

10 The following day the public was indignant. CBS said it might drop *The Mercury Theatre on the Air* from its lineup. Perhaps even more frightening than a real alien invasion was a proposal by Senator Herring of Iowa that all future radio broadcasts be reviewed by the government before presentation.

11 Many lawsuits were prepared, but the radio network was able to defend itself by pointing to the multiple announcements made during the program reminding listeners that what they were hearing was a radio drama. In the end, the major effect of the broadcast was to increase the ratings of *The Mercury Theatre on the Air* and catapult Orson Welles's career further forward.

12 Why did it affect people so deeply? It may have been because the "live" bulletin seemed to interrupt the news, confusing people about what was real and what was not. The public was undoubtedly also jittery because of the political situation in Europe. In only six more years, the United States would be drawn into World War II. Just a month before, a crisis in Munich had been covered on the radio with the same type of bulletins used in the broadcast.

13 Could it happen again? Many suggest that the public is now much too sensible and media-savvy to be fooled by such a hoax. But consider this: In September of 1996 hundreds of people in Madrid, Spain were panicked by television "news" broadcasts depicting giant saucers hovering over United States landmarks. They actually believed the newscast. The segments turned out to be clever advertisements for an alien invasion movie, *Independence Day*.

Looking at Language

1 • Identify five cognates or false cognates in Paragraph 13. Beside each choice, determine if the meaning is the same or different in your language.

WORD IN ENGLISH	WORD IN YOUR LANGUAGE	MEANING	
		Same	Different

Comprehension

2 • What techniques did Welles use to make the Martian attack seem realistic?

____

____

3 • Was Welles purposely trying to cause citizens to panic? Explain your answer and find a supporting quotation from the text.

____

____

____

4 • Why were people so ready to believe in the Martian invasion? Think of three reasons.

____

____

____

____

5 • In Paragraph 10, why does the author call Senator Herring's proposal more frightening than an alien invasion? You'll have to make a guess.

____

____

6 • What does "The Night the Martians Attacked" tell us about human nature?

____

____

7 • In your opinion, are people today less easily manipulated by the media, or are they as gullible as people were in 1938? Think of a specific example to support your point.

____

____

____

Discussion

When events are widely reported, mass hysteria may occur. What recent events have caused people to panic?

Speaking •• Create a Radio Play

To practise your speaking skills, visit the companion website.

Work with a partner or a small team of students and prepare a short radio play about a hoax. You can get ideas from tabloid newspapers. For example, you could present a story about a strange new species, alien messages, an invasion of killer bugs, fish falling from the sky, hidden cameras in televisions, or any other exciting, frightening, or unusual event. Use your imagination!

Present your play as if it were a news story. If it is appropriate for your story, you could use sound effects during your play. Remember that everyday objects are very effective for the creation of sound effects. For example, if you wear gloves and rub gravel on the ground, it sounds like a car on a road. Discover what sounds will make your production more interesting.

Watching •• JFK: What's Fact, What's Not

When filmmakers attempt to retell historical events, they are invariably accused of manipulating the facts to present a biased point of view. One film, in particular, was attacked because it attempted to answer one of the biggest mysteries of the twentieth century. Oliver Stone, in his film *JFK*, tackled the question, "Who killed John Fitzgerald Kennedy?" What really happened on November 22, 1963, at 12:30 p.m.?

Pre-Watching Discussion

1 • With your classmates, discuss what you already know about the assassination.

2 • Review the following information.

JOHN F. KENNEDY	He was the youngest president of the United States. He was visiting Dallas prior to his 1964 re-election campaign.
LEE HARVEY OSWALD	He was a U.S. citizen and former Marine. After a brief period living in Russia, Oswald got a job at the Book Depository in Dallas.
LYNDON JOHNSON	He was the vice-president and the man who took over the government after Kennedy was assassinated.
WARREN COMMISSION	This commission, named after Justice Earl Warren, was set up after the assassination to determine what had happened.

Watching Comprehension

1 • List some facts and theories about the assassination.

	WARREN COMMISSION	CONSPIRACY THEORISTS
Who killed Kennedy?	Oswald	The communists
The bullets that hit Kennedy came from which direction?	6th floor of a building behind	
How many shots were fired?	3	

2 • Who killed Lee Harvey Oswald? Jack Ruby

3 • How many seconds did the shooting of Kennedy last? 6 seconds

4 • Why was one bullet called "magic"? Because it had hit Connell and Kennedy. and the bullet is almost perfect after

5 • What suspicious events involved Kennedy's body when it was transported to Washington?

That someone ~~changed the body~~ changed the casket and they were surgery done

6 • Why was the photo of Oswald holding a gun suspicious? His head looked like it was pasted on it

7 • What did eyewitnesses say about the locations of the gunshots? They think it was from the ~~[illegible]~~ grassy Knoll

8 • The Warren Commission report concluded that the same bullet hit Kennedy and Governor Connally. Why does Governor Connally disagree?

He had time to turn around

Discussion

1 • According to the evidence presented in the video, was Oswald the lone assassin of President Kennedy?

2 • Will the truth ever come out about the Kennedy assassination? Why or why not?

3 • In a *New York Times* article, Stephen E. Ambrose claimed that conspiracy theories are linked to political agendas. What other conspiracy theories do you know about?

4 • Could conspiracy theories be dangerous? Explain why.

Writing Topics

Write a composition about one of the following topics. Remember to include a thesis statement and provide supporting examples. Before handing in your work, refer to the Writing Checklist on the inside back cover.

1 • Argue that toys do or do not reinforce gender stereotypes.

2 • Are toy guns, swords, knives, and violent video games bad for children? Explain your views.

To review some of the vocabulary studied in this chapter, visit the companion website.

3 • Should advertising to children be banned? Explain how advertisers manipulate children. You can refer to your own experiences and to information found in this chapter.

4 • Prove that people are easily influenced by the media. You can refer to popular advertising, the Orson Welles radio drama, and other examples of mass hysteria.

5 • Argue that John F. Kennedy was or was not killed by Lee Harvey Oswald. You can use evidence from the video *JFK: What's Fact, What's Not.*

CHAPTER 5

•• The palest ink is better than the best memory. ••

Chinese proverb

The Memory Wars

Police departments and courtrooms rely on the memory of witnesses. But how reliable and stable is memory? This chapter examines how the human mind can be manipulated.

Warm Up •• Using Description

Take a look at the four photos. Then close your book and describe some of the things that you saw. Use descriptive words and phrases.

(Note to teachers: Please refer to the Teacher's Annotated Edition for further instructions about this activity.)

A

B

C

D

Watching •• Unreliable Evidence

You may see dozens of different faces on any given day. But how many can you really remember? Dr. Rod Lindsay is an expert in eyewitness identification. You will view a report about the reliability of eyewitness testimony.

Watching Comprehension

1 • How old was Marvin Anderson when he was convicted of rape? ____________

2 • What were two problems with the photo lineup that was shown to the rape victim?

____

____

____

3 • According to Dr. Rod Lindsay, how should a photo lineup be presented?

____

____

____

4 • What is the double-blind procedure? ______________________________

____

5 • Lindsay contacted 33 police departments. How many use the double-blind procedure?

____

6 • How do sequential lineups of photos reduce witness identification error?

____

____

7 • Of the 33 police departments that were contacted, how many use sequential lineups of photos?

____

8 • In his class, Doctor Lindsay has 42 students who eyewitnessed his "shooting." How many students correctly identified the perpetrator?

____

9 • According to Dr. Lindsay, between 40 and 300 innocent people will be convicted this year based on faulty eyewitness testimony. Why will so many be convicted? Think of three reasons.

____

____

____

____

To work on your writing skills, visit the companion website.

10 • Why was Marvin Anderson eventually exonerated and freed? ____________

____

Discussion

1 • Professor Lindsay's experimental method with his students was later criticized by the media. Why do you think he was criticized?

2 • During criminal trials, should eyewitness testimony be discounted? Why or why not?

Tip Grammar

Memory, *Remind*, and *Souvenir*

Memory is a noun meaning "the capacity to retain past impressions." It can also refer to the past impressions themselves.

Remind is a verb meaning "to cause a person to remember something."

A *souvenir* is a memento that you buy to remind yourself of a special place.

> When we went to New York, we brought back a **souvenir** of the Statue of Liberty. Please **remind** me to call my grandmother and tell her about it. She is eighty, but she has a great **memory**. She has fond **memories** of the first time she saw the Statue of Liberty.

You can practise using these terms in *Open Road English Grammar*, Unit 12.

Reading

Reading Strategy

Summarizing

A summary is a review of a text's main ideas. When you summarize, you restate what the author said using your own words.

How to Summarize

1 • **Identify the source, in other words, the author and the title of the text that you are summarizing.** Include this information in the first sentence of your summary.

2 • **State the main idea.** Using your own words, explain what the author's main idea is. Do not copy from the original text.

3 • **Select the most important ideas.** Read the text and write down the key information. Only write down single words, names, or dates. Do not write down phrases or entire sentences. Then, in your own words, explain the author's supporting points. (To avoid plagiarizing, it is a good idea to put the original text aside and to write your summary from memory.)

4 • **Verify that you have not copied exact phrases or sentences** from the original text.

5 • **Do not express an opinion.** Your summary should present the author's ideas, not your own, unless your teacher specifically asks for your opinion.

Original Source

Twenty-five years of research have taught Dr. Frances Aboud what works in building tolerance, and what doesn't. What does not work, she says, is the nominal mixing of the tribes. "It's not just integrating the schools, where you put them together," she says. "You have to have them in the same class, intensively working on projects in mixed pairs or in mixed groups. Having a succession of cross-race friends—friends you respect and trust—has a positive impact later on. But it's got to be more than one [friend], and it's got to be at the level of real co-operative learning and working together."

From "P Is for Prejudice" by Allen Abel

Summary

In Allen Abel's article "P is for Prejudice," the author describes Dr. Frances Aboud's racism reseach. Dr. Aboud suggests that the best way to create a more open-minded population is to mix different races together in schools so that people can work together and create friendships.

Tip

Avoid Plagiarism!

Plagiarism is the act of using someone else's words or ideas without giving that person credit. Plagiarism is a very serious offence.

The following actions are examples of plagiarism:

- copying another person's work and presenting it as your own
- failing to use quotation marks to properly set off an author's exact words
- using ideas from another source without citing that source
- making slight modifications to an author's sentences, but presenting the work as your own

To avoid plagiarism, always cite the source when you borrow words, phrases, or ideas from an author.

Reading Exercise 1

Read the following selections and answer the questions. The original selection, written by Saundra K. Ciccarelli, appeared in *Psychology* on page 214.

Original Selection

Although it is rare, some people do have what is properly called *eidetic imagery*, or the ability to access a visual memory over a long period of time. The popular term *photographic memory* is often used to mean

this rare ability. People with eidetic imagery ability might be able to look quickly at a page in a book, and then by focusing on a blank wall, "read" the words from the image that still lingers in their sensory memory ... Although it might sound like a great ability to have while in college, it actually provides little advantage when taking tests, because it's just like having an open-book test. If a student can't understand what's written on the pages, having the book open is useless.

Summary 1

In *Psychology*, Saundra K. Ciccarelli writes that some people have eidetic imagery ability, also known as photographic memory, which is the ability to access a visual memory over a long period. However, the ability is not very useful during test-taking because a person may be able to recall, but not understand, what is written on a page.

1 • How does this summary plagiarize the original piece of writing?

____

____

Summary 2

The technical term for photographic memory is eidetic imagery ability. People with this ability can scan a page and remember the details on the page at a later point in time.

2 • How does this summary plagiarize the original piece of writing?

____

____

Reading Exercise 2

Read the following sentences and then summarize what the author said. Your summary can be two or three sentences.

And so, it is an unsettling fact that we can manufacture, wholesale and out of pure nothingness, whole events and pasts that never occurred. This fantastical creative ability of our minds may be treasured when it produces *King Lear* or *War and Peace*, but it can sometimes destroy lives and families when applied to ordinary, daily life. When it comes to legal cases—and the fate of a defendant—precise memory about even the tiniest of details can be crucial.

From "The Memory Wars" by Elizabeth Loftus

____

____

____

____

____

Reading 5.1

Sometimes the battle for truth in science comes at great personal cost. Elizabeth Loftus knows that first-hand. Her decades of research showed that memory—whether eyewitness testimony in a court or our most private and personal recollections—is malleable and easily distorted. But these discoveries landed her in the middle of a cultural war. As you read, highlight the main ideas. Later, you will summarize this text.

The Memory Wars

by Elizabeth Loftus

1 Memory is a paradox, both the key to unlocking the self and a veil that forever hides the self. Memory selects the narrative that helps us cohere and make sense of ourselves. And yet, for both individuals and cultures, those narratives sometimes **rend** us, distort us, and lead to tragedies like war. Memory is the bedrock of self, and yet, as my research has conclusively shown, it is utterly malleable, selective, and changing. Perhaps it is the richness of memory that has kept it such a fascinating topic for me for my entire life.

2 I first discovered the perturbing truth about the malleable nature of memory when I began to experimentally study the human mind. In studies I conducted in the 1970s and 1980s, I showed what can happen when a person sees a crime or an accident and is later questioned about the experience in a biased way. "How fast were the cars going when they smashed into each other?" led the accident witnesses to estimate the speed as higher than those who had been asked a more neutral question, like "How fast were the cars going when they hit each other?" Moreover, the "smashed" question led more people to later falsely recall they had seen broken glass, when no glass was broken at all.

3 In another study, a simple leading question that referred to a barn made some people come to believe they had seen a barn in a bucolic scene that contained no buildings at all. It was utterly surprising to watch as people reported they had seen something that would have been large and conspicuous if it actually had been there. It's a scary thing to think that our memories might be so malleable. Yet today, hundreds of studies have documented how exposure to misinformation can distort our memories. We pick up misinformation when we are interrogated in a suggestive way, or when we talk with other people who give an erroneous version of a past event.

4 It's not just memory for small details that is pliable and easily manipulated. Our memory systems are capable of creating in unsuspecting minds whole events that never happened. People even claim to recall experiences that would be virtually impossible, such as a woman I'll call Meg who "remembered" in excruciating detail acts of parental abuse that allegedly occurred when she was six months old—which is, from all our evidence of how and when memories form, an impossibility. This is an example of what many psychological scientists would call "false memory."

 rend tear

5 Memory is malleable, and the real question is: How can we best live with that truth? *False memory. Repressed memory. Recovered memory.* These were the rallying calls for an entire generation of therapists, patients, and families. Cases like that of Meg erupted on the scene of American culture, with countless adults "recovering" memories of abuse in therapy, with middle-aged parents suddenly being accused of crimes they were sure they had never committed, and with sensationalist court trials where more than a few innocent people went to jail.

6 In the midst of all this cultural ferment, on the fault lines of a war over the nature of memory, I stood with my studies. My first research in generating false memories used a technique whereby the relatives of subjects were enlisted to help create scenarios describing true childhood events (such as getting a fire truck on the sixth birthday) and a false one (getting lost for an extended time in a shopping mall and ultimately being rescued by an elderly person). We fed the scenarios to subjects, claiming they were all true. After three suggestive interviews, about a quarter of these subjects came to believe, wholly or partially, that they had been lost in this way. Many added embellishing details to their accounts, such as descriptions of the person who rescued them.

7 Today, many other investigators have used the "lost-in the-mall" technique to plant false memories of events that would have been far more unusual, bizarre, or traumatic had they actually happened. Subjects have been led to believe that they had an accident at a family wedding as a child, that they nearly drowned and had to be rescued by a lifeguard, or that they had once been victims of a vicious animal attack. In some instances, individuals develop very rich false memories; they feel confident, provide details, and even express emotion about the false events that never really happened.

8 And so, it is an unsettling fact that we can manufacture, wholesale and out of pure nothingness, whole events and pasts that never occurred. This fantastical creative ability of our minds may be treasured when it produces *King Lear* or *War and Peace*, but it can sometimes destroy lives and families when applied to ordinary, daily life. When it comes to legal cases—and the fate of a defendant—precise memory about even the tiniest of details can be crucial.

9 What happens when a scientist stumbles into the middle of a hot and furious cultural war? I found that raising questions about the authenticity of memory—particularly memories of sexual abuse—was the perfect recipe for an unpopularity contest. In fact, my own life has been derailed by the response to my research, oddly akin to the lives of some of those on whose behalf I testify. My research, and the publicity surrounding the more notorious court cases, triggered an explosion of hostility that initially caught me by surprise. Along with threatening letters, people tried to get professional organizations to rescind their invitations to have me speak. At some universities, armed guards were provided to accompany me during invited speeches after people called to threaten harm if the talks were not cancelled. I was accused of molesting my own children, even though I don't have any children.

10 Sometimes the truths science uncovers are not easy, simple, or reassuring. After publishing his "Dialogue Concerning the Two Chief World Systems," Galileo was found guilty of heresy and confined to house arrest. Galileo worked hard to convince his generation that earth was not solidly fixed in the centre of the universe. Likewise, memory researchers have worked hard to convince a skeptical public that memory is not solidly fixed in the centre of our minds. A popular mythology has Galileo saying, "Nevertheless it moves," as he arose from his knees before the Inquisition. I might paraphrase this fictitious Galileo and say, "Nevertheless memory moves."

To practise your speaking skills, visit the companion website.

Written Response

Write your responses on a separate sheet of paper.

1 • Identify and define five difficult terms from this text.

2 • Summarize this essay. Follow the rules of summary writing found on pages 55 and 56.

Listening •• Crime Scene Witness

The traditional domain of the prosecutor is the courtroom, but a new project is changing that. Susan Helenchilde is Canada's first community prosecutor. It's a role that takes her out of the hallowed halls of justice and onto the streets of Winnipeg. Listen to the interview.

Listening Comprehension

1 • In two or three sentences, describe what happened to the "good Samaritan."

____

____

____

____

2 • Are the following sentences true or false? If you think any statement is false, write a true statement under it.

a) The attacker had a previous history of violence........................ T F

____

b) The good Samaritan was alone in the world and had no family...... T F

____

c) The woman who was initially harassed by the attacker got on a bus and left the scene... T F

____

3 • Who was commonly known as Santa Claus?

a) the attacker b) the victim

4 • What happened to the victim?

a) He died from his injuries.

b) He suffered brain damage and will have to live in a nursing home for the rest of his life.

c) He was badly hurt, but he is okay now.

To develop your listening skills, visit the companion website.

5 • Bob Rheume was the star witness. What did he do when he saw the attack?

____

6 • According to Susan Helenchilde, why do witnesses leave crime scenes?

____

____

7 • Two witnesses, a brother and sister, initially said, "We didn't see anything," yet when the police questioned them again, the sister's information helped the prosecution. What did she see?

____

____

8 • How did the sister's evidence help the case?

____

____

9 • What is the prosecutor's advice to crime witnesses?

____

____

Speaking •• Memory Techniques

You will learn some simple memory techniques.

1 • Your teacher will read aloud two lists of numbers. Write down the numbers that you remember.

2 • Try to memorize the names of the five Great Lakes, which lie between Canada and the United States. Look at the names for ten seconds and then cover this page.

Erie	Michigan	Ontario	Superior	Huron

3 • Spend about ten seconds trying to memorize the words below. Then, on a separate piece of paper, write down as many words as you can remember.

lonely	hat	toaster	kick	cat	knife
coat	bread	woman	sleep	floor	jam

Reading

Reading 5.2

How accurate are our memories of the past? In the following essay, excerpted from his collection entitled *Me Talk Pretty One Day,* David Sedaris contrasts his own childhood with that of his friend who lived in Africa.

My African Childhood

by David Sedaris

1 When Hugh was in the fifth grade, his class took a field trip to an Ethiopian slaughterhouse. He was living in Addis Ababa at the time, and the slaughterhouse was chosen because, he says, "it was convenient." This was a school system in which the matter of proximity outweighed such petty concerns as what may or may not be appropriate for a busload of eleven-year-olds. "What?" I asked. "Were there no autopsies scheduled at the local morgue? Was the federal prison just a bit too far out of the way?"

2 Hugh defends his former school, saying, "Well, isn't that the whole point of a field trip? To see something new?"

3 "Technically yes, but ..."

4 "All right then," he says. "So we saw some new things." One of his field trips was literally a trip to a field where the class watched a wrinkled man fill his mouth with rotten goat meat and feed it to a pack of waiting hyenas. On another occasion they were taken to examine the bloodied bedroom curtains hanging in the palace of the former dictator. There were tamer trips, to textile factories and sugar refineries, but my favourite is always the slaughterhouse. It wasn't a big company, just a small rural enterprise run by a couple of brothers operating out of a low-ceilinged concrete building. Following a brief lecture on the importance of proper sanitation, a small white piglet was herded into the room, its dainty hooves clicking against the concrete floor. The class gathered in a circle to get a better look at the animal, who seemed delighted with the attention he was getting. He turned from face to face and was looking up at Hugh when one of the brothers drew a pistol from his back pocket, held it against the animal's temple, and shot the piglet, execution-style. Blood spattered, frightened children wept, and the man with the gun offered the teacher and bus driver some meat from a freshly slaughtered goat.

5 When I'm told such stories, it's all I can do to hold back my feelings of jealousy. An Ethiopian slaughterhouse. Some people have all the luck. When I was in elementary school, the best we ever got was a trip to Old Salem or Colonial Williamsburg, one of those preserved brick villages where time supposedly stands still, and someone earns his living as a town crier. There was always a blacksmith, a group of wandering patriots, and a collection of bonneted women hawking cornbread or gingersnaps made "the old fashioned way." Every now and then you might come across a doer of bad deeds serving time in the stocks, but that was generally as exciting as it got.

6 Certain events are parallel, but compared with Hugh's, my childhood was unspeakably dull. When I was seven years old, my family moved to North Carolina. When he was seven years old, Hugh's family moved to the Congo. We had a collie and a house cat. They had a monkey and two horses named Charlie Brown and Satan. I threw stones at stop signs. Hugh threw stones at crocodiles. The verbs are the same, but he definitely wins the

prize when it comes to nouns and objects. An eventful day for my mother might have involved a trip to the dry cleaner or a conversation with the potato-chip deliveryman. Asked one ordinary Congo afternoon what she'd done with her day, Hugh's mother answered that she and a fellow member of the Ladies' Club had visited a leper colony on the outskirts of Kinshasa. No reason was given for the expedition, though chances are she was staking it out for a future field trip.

7 Due to his upbringing, Hugh sits through inane movies never realizing that they're often based on inane television shows. There were no poker-faced sitcom Martians in his part of Africa, no oil-rich hillbillies or aproned brides trying to wean themselves from the practice of **witchcraft**. From time to time a movie would arrive packed in a dented canister, the film scratched and faded from its slow trip around the world. The theatre consisted of a few dozen folding chairs arranged before a bed sheet or the blank wall of a vacant hangar out near the airstrip. Occasionally a man would sell warm soft drinks out of a cardboard box, but that was it in terms of concessions.

8 When I was young, I went to the theatre at the nearby shopping centre and watched a movie about a talking Volkswagen. I believe the little car had a taste for mischief but I can't be certain, as both the movie and the afternoon proved unremarkable and have faded from my memory. Hugh saw the same movie a few years after it was released. His family had left the Congo by this time and were living in Ethiopia. Like me, Hugh saw the movie by himself on a weekend afternoon. Unlike me, he left the theatre two hours later to find a dead man hanging from a telephone pole at the far end of the unpaved parking lot. None of the people who'd seen the movie seemed to care about the dead man. They stared at him for a moment or two and then headed home, saying they'd never seen anything as crazy as that talking Volkswagen. His father was late picking him up, so Hugh just stood there for an hour, watching the dead man dangle and turn in the breeze. The death was not reported in the newspaper, and when Hugh related the story to his friends, they said, "You saw the movie about the talking car?"

9 I could have done without the flies and the primitive theatres, but I wouldn't have minded growing up with a houseful of servants. In North Carolina, it wasn't unusual to have a once-a-week maid, but Hugh's family had houseboys, a word that never fails to charge my imagination. They had cooks and drivers, and guards who occupied a gatehouse, armed with machetes. Seeing as I had regularly petitioned my parents for an electric fence, the business with the guards strikes me as the last word in quiet sophistication. Having protection suggests that you are important. Having that protection paid for by the government is even better, as it suggests your safety is of interest to someone other than yourself.

10 Hugh's father was a career officer with the U.S. State Department, and every morning a black sedan carried him off to the embassy. I'm told it's not as glamorous as it sounds, but in terms of fun for the entire family, I'm fairly confident that it beats the sack race at the annual IBM picnic. By the age of three, Hugh was already carrying a diplomatic passport. The rules that applied to others did not apply to him. No tickets, no arrests, no luggage search: He was officially licensed to act like a brat. Being an American, it was expected of him, and who was he to deny the world an occasional tantrum?

11 They weren't rich, but what Hugh's family lacked financially they more than made up for with the sort of exoticism that works wonders at cocktail parties, leading always to the remark, "That sounds fascinating." It's a compliment one rarely receives when describing an

•• **witchcraft** The references are to the television shows *My Favorite Martian*, *The Beverly Hillbillies*, and *Bewitched*.

adolescence spent drinking **Icees** at the North Hills Mall. No fifteen-foot python ever wandered onto my school's basketball court. I begged, I prayed nightly, but it just never happened. Neither did I get to witness a military coup in which forces sympathetic to the colonel arrived late at night to assassinate my next-door neighbour. Hugh had been at the Addis Ababa teen club when the electricity was cut off and soldiers arrived to evacuate the building. He and his friends had to hide in the back of a jeep and cover themselves with blankets during the ride home. It's something that sticks in his mind for one reason or another.

12 Among my personal highlights is the memory of having my picture taken with Uncle Paul, the legally blind host of a Raleigh children's television show. Among Hugh's is the memory of having his picture taken with Buzz Aldrin on the last leg of the astronaut's world tour. The man who had walked on the moon placed his hand on Hugh's shoulder and offered to sign his autograph book. The man who led Wake County schoolchildren in afternoon song turned at the sound of my voice and asked, "So what's your name, princess?"

13 When I was fourteen years old, I was sent to spend ten days with my maternal grandmother in western New York State. She was a small and private woman named Billie, and though she never came right out and asked, I had the distinct impression she had no idea who I was. It was the way she looked at me, squinting through her glasses while chewing on her lower lip. That, coupled with the fact that she never once called me by name. "Oh," she'd say, "are you still here?" She was just beginning her long struggle with Alzheimer's disease, and each time I entered the room, I felt the need to reintroduce myself and set her at ease. "Hi, it's me. Sharon's boy, David. I was just in the kitchen admiring your collection of ceramic toads." Aside from a few trips to summer camp, this was the longest I'd ever been away from home, and I like to think I was toughened by the experience.

14 About the same time I was frightening my grandmother, Hugh and his family were packing their belongings for a move to Somalia. There were no English-speaking schools in Mogadishu, so, after a few months spent lying around the family compound with his pet monkey, Hugh was sent back to Ethiopia to live with a beer enthusiast his father had met at a cocktail party. Mr. Hoyt installed security systems in foreign embassies. He and his family gave Hugh a room. They invited him to join them at the table, but that was as far as they extended themselves. No one ever asked him when his birthday was, so when the day came, he kept it to himself. There was no telephone service between Ethiopia and Somalia, and letters to his parents were sent to Washington and then forwarded on to Mogadishu, meaning that his news was more than a month old by the time they got it. I suppose it wasn't much different than living as a foreign-exchange student. Young people do it all the time, but to me it sounds awful. The Hoyts had two sons about Hugh's age who were always saying things like "Hey that's *our* sofa you're sitting on" and "Hands off that ornamental stein. It doesn't belong to you."

15 He'd been living with these people for a year when he overheard Mr. Hoyt tell a friend that he and his family would soon be moving to Munich, Germany, the beer capital of the world. "And that worried me," Hugh said, "because it meant I'd have to find some other place to live."

16 Where I come from, finding shelter is a problem the average teenager might confidently leave to his parents. It was just something that came with having a mom and a dad. Worried that he might be sent to live with his grandparents in Kentucky, Hugh turned to the school's guidance counsellor, who knew of a family whose son had recently left for college. And so he spent another year living with strangers and not mentioning his

•• **Icees** frozen carbonated beverages

birthday. While I wouldn't have wanted to do it myself, I can't help but envy the sense of fortitude he gained from the experience. After graduating from college, he moved to France knowing only the phrase "Do you speak French?"—a question guaranteed to get you nowhere unless you also speak the language.

17 While living in Africa, Hugh and his family took frequent vacations, often in the company of their monkey. The Nairobi Hilton, some suite of high-ceilinged rooms in Cairo or Khartoum: These are the places his people recall when gathered at a common table. "Was that the summer we spent in Beirut or, no, I'm thinking of the time we sailed from Cyprus and took the Orient Express to Istanbul."

18 Theirs was the life I dreamed about during my vacations in eastern North Carolina. Hugh's family was hobnobbing with chiefs and sultans while I ate hush puppies at the Sanitary Fish Market in Morehead City, a beach towel wrapped like a *hijab* around my head. Someone unknown to me was very likely standing in a muddy ditch and dreaming of an evening spent sitting in a clean family restaurant, drinking iced tea and working his way through an extra-large seaman's platter, but that did not concern me, as it meant I should have been happy with what I had.

19 Rather than surrender to my bitterness, I have learned to take satisfaction in the life that Hugh has led. His stories have, over time, become my own. I say this with no trace of a ***kumbaya***. There is no spiritual symbiosis; I'm just a petty thief who lifts his memories the same way I'll take a handful of change left on his dresser. When my own experiences fall short of the mark, I just go out and spend some of his. It is with pleasure that I sometimes recall the dead man's purple face or the report of the handgun ringing in my ears as I studied the blood pooling beneath the dead white piglet. On the way back from the slaughterhouse, we stopped for Cokes in the village of Mojo, where the gas-station owner had arranged a few tables and chairs beneath a dying canopy of vines. It was late afternoon by the time we returned to school, where a second bus carried me to the foot of Coffeeboard Road. Once there, I walked through a grove of eucalyptus trees and alongside a bald pasture of starving cattle, past the guard napping in his gatehouse, and into the warm arms of my monkey.

•• **kumbaya** from a spiritual song, denotes naive optimism

Comprehension and Critical Thinking

1 • What is the meaning of *inane* in Paragraph 7?

a) fascinating **b)** serious **c)** ridiculous

2 • David Sedaris compares his childhood to Hugh's. Briefly describe Sedaris's childhood. Give a few details.

____

____

3 • How were the author's school field trips different from Hugh's?

____

____

____

____

4 • In Paragraph 13, the author describes the time he spent with his grandmother, and in Paragraph 14, he describes Hugh's year with the Hoyt family. What are some similarities and differences in their experiences?

____

____

____

____

5 • In Paragraph 4, the author describes Hugh's trip to a slaughterhouse. In Paragraph 8, he describes Hugh's trip to a theatre, and in Paragraph 11, he discusses a military coup that Hugh witnessed. What do the anecdotes about Hugh's childhood have in common?

____

____

6 • On the surface, the author appears to envy Hugh's childhood. Yet what were some of the disadvantages of Hugh's childhood?

____

____

____

7 • In the conclusion, Sedaris writes that he is "a petty thief who lifts [Hugh's] memories." Why does he steal Hugh's memories?

____

____

____

Written Response

1 • In a paragraph, explain who probably had the better childhood: David Sedaris or his friend Hugh.

2 • Compose ten questions about "My African Childhood."

Writing Topics

Write a composition about one of the following topics. Remember to include a thesis statement and provide supporting examples. Before handing in your work, refer to the Writing Checklist on the inside back cover.

To review some of the vocabulary studied in this chapter, visit the companion website.

1 • How is eyewitness testimony unreliable? You can quote from "The Memory Wars" and you can give examples from the video "Unreliable Evidence."

2 • Describe some mistakes police departments make that can lead to wrongful convictions. You can give examples from the video "Unreliable Evidence."

3 • Write an essay comparing and contrasting the typical childhood of someone in your culture or age group with that of someone from another culture or age group. To prepare for this activity, conduct an interview with someone who grew up during a different era or whose childhood occurred in another country.

CHAPTER 6

Conscience

•• Many would be cowards if they had courage enough. ••

Thomas Fuller

Throughout history, humans have found reasons to attack and harm each other. This chapter examines the influence of social roles on aggression.

Warm Up •• Moments in Time

There are historical moments that become frozen in time. People who lived through a startling moment generally recollect where they were when the event happened.

Look at the following list of historical moments. Most occurred before you were born. With a partner or a team of students, try to identify as many of the following historical moments as possible.

1 • 1867. North American colonies united to create a new nation.	______________________
2 • 1891. An Ontario-born physical education teacher invented this sport using a soccer ball and two peach baskets.	______________________
3 • 1903. She became the first woman to win the Nobel Prize.	______________________
4 • April 15, 1912. It was considered unsinkable. Then it sank.	______________________
5 • June 28, 1914. The assassination of Archduke Franz Ferdinand precipitated this event.	______________________
6 • October 24, 1929. This crash was heard around the world.	______________________
7 • December 11, 1936. In order to marry a divorced American woman, Britain's King Edward VIII made a shocking decision.	______________________
8 • November 9, 1938. The sound of breaking glass foretold the horrors to come.	______________________
9 • December 7, 1941. This moment, said Roosevelt, "will live in infamy."	______________________
10 • August 6, 1945. "Little Boy" dropped on a Japanese city.	______________________

11 • 1947. Tommy Douglas, the Saskatchewan premier, launched this system. ______

12 • January 30, 1948. This spiritual leader was a stirring symbol of non-violence, and he died violently. ______

13 • May 14, 1948. A homeland at last. ______

14 • Fall 1949. China laid claim to this independent Buddhist nation. ______

15 • August 5, 1962. She sang a birthday song to the president; then on this day her candle burned out. ______

16 • April 4, 1968. The greatest voice for civil rights was killed. ______

17 • July 20, 1969. His giant leap was actually one small step. ______

18 • May 1977. A new music movement began with the song "God Save the Queen." The cover of the single featured a picture of the Queen of England with a safety pin through her nose. ______

19 • July 25, 1978. Baby Louise was born and made medical history. ______

20 • December 8, 1980. A deluded gunman killed a legendary former Beatle near Central Park in New York. ______

21 • May 11, 1981. This Jamaican reggae star tragically succumbed to the cancer that had begun as a small melanoma on his toe. ______

22 • June 4, 1989. In China, tanks rolled over protesters. ______

23 • November 9, 1989. This structure that had divided a city came tumbling down. ______

24 • April 8, 1994. A frail, talented, former "teen spirit" was found dead at his Seattle mansion. ______

25 • January 1997. A sheep hit the headlines and began an ethical debate. ______

26 • July 2000. Long after the revolution, decades of one-party rule finally ended in this democratic North American nation. ______

27 • September 11, 2001. Towers toppled. ______

28 • December 26, 2004. An underwater earthquake caused entire villages to disappear. ______

To work on your writing skills, visit the companion website.

Discussion

1 • What three events in the list are the most historically important and will be remembered hundreds of years from now?

2 • What world events that took place in the past five years could become frozen moments in time?

Reading

Reading 6.1

In the 1960s, Stanley Milgram developed a psychological study designed to test people's willingness to hurt others. You may have heard about the experiment. But why did some people in the experiment choose to resist authority? Read about one participant's motivations.

Resisting Authority

by Joseph Dimow

1 In 1961, I participated in a famous experimental study about obedience and authority—although I and other participants were led to believe it was a study of memory and learning. The experiment was designed by a Yale University professor of social psychology, Stanley Milgram, and resulted in a book, *Obedience to Authority*, which is still widely used in sociology courses.

2 Like many others in the New Haven area, I answered an ad seeking subjects for the experiment and offering five dollars for travel and time. At the Yale facility, I met a man who looked very professorial in a white coat and horn-rimmed glasses. He led me into a room filled with an impressive display of electrical equipment. A second man was introduced to me as another subject for the experiment, and together we were told that the experiment was to test the widely held belief that people learn by punishment. In this case, one of us would be a "learner" and the other a "teacher." The teacher would read a list of paired words to the learner and then repeat the first word of the pair. If the learner did not respond with the correct second word, the teacher would deliver a "mild" electric shock to the learner as punishment. This struck me as bizarre, and although the instructions were in accord with what we had been told, I wondered if something else was going on.

3 The "professor" said we would draw straws to see which of us would be the learner. He offered the straws to the other man and then announced that he had drawn the short straw and would be the learner. I hadn't seen either straw, and my doubts became suspicions that I was being deceived.

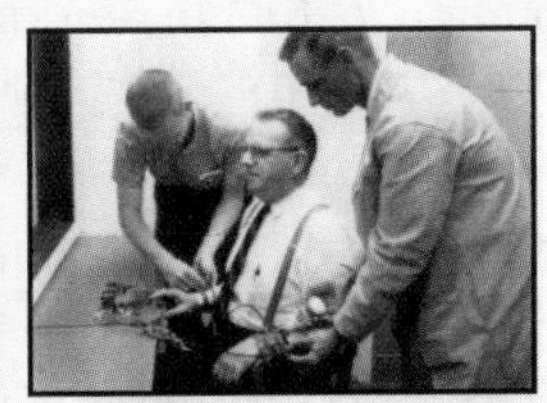

4 The learner, said the professor, would be in an adjoining room, out of my sight, and strapped to a chair so that his arms could not move—this so that the learner could not jump around and damage the equipment or do harm to himself. I was to be seated in front of a console marked with lettering coloured yellow for "Slight Shock" (15 volts) up to purple for "Danger: Severe Shock" (450 volts). The shocks would increase by 15-volt increments with each incorrect answer.

5 I was very suspicious and asked a number of questions: *Isn't it dangerous? How do you know the learner doesn't have a bad heart and can't take the shocks? What if he wants to stop? Can he get out of the chair?* The professor assured me that the shocks were not painful or harmful.

6 I asked the learner if he was willing to do this and why he didn't have any questions. He said, "Let's try it." With some trepidation on my part, we began the experiment.

7 After a few shocks, the learner let out an "Ouch!" and I asked if he was okay. He said he was, but after the next shock, his complaint became louder. I said I would stop. The professor told me to continue, and the learner said he was ready to go on, too. I went on for two or three more shocks. With each, the learner's cry of pain became louder—and then he asked to stop, and I refused to go any further.

8 The professor became very authoritative. He said that I was costing them valuable time, it was essential for me to continue, and I was ruining the experiment. He asserted that he was in charge, not me. He reminded me that I had been paid and insisted that I continue. I refused, offered to give him back the five dollars, and told him that I believed the experiment to be really about how far I would go, that the learner was an accomplice, and that I was determined not to continue.

9 At that point, the professor gave up and his demeanour changed. Instead of being authoritative and assertive, he was detached and polite as he asked if I would answer some questions about what had taken place. I agreed, and he asked a series of questions about who was responsible for what had happened.

10 After several questions, I asked if my suspicions were correct and if the whole experiment was designed to see if ordinary Americans would obey immoral orders, as many Germans had done during the Nazi period. The professor declined to answer, but asked what had made me think that the experiment was not what had been described to me at the beginning. I told him that my suspicions had been aroused by the way the straws had been handled, by the idea that they would risk shocking a stranger, and by the fact that he, the professor, had been in the area with me the whole time and had never gone to observe the learner. He did not respond to my comments, but said I would receive a report when the experiment was completed.

11 Months later, the report that I received confirmed that the experiment was designed to see how far subjects would go in obeying orders to administer pain to others. It had arisen out of the desire to understand the widespread obedience to horrendous and brutal orders in Nazi Germany. The report also confirmed that the professor and learner were indeed actors.

12 Of forty participants in Milgram's first experiment, fifteen refused to continue at some point, while twenty-five went all the way to 450 volts—a "shock" that they administered three times before the experiment was ended by the professor. (There was no actual shock, of course. The actor playing the part of the learner reacted with a cry of pain to a red light, which lit whenever there was a supposed shock.)

13 The experiment was repeated in other venues away from the university in Hartford and Cambridge. Results were the worst (that is, the highest percentage of testers went all the

way to 450 volts) with a group of nurses in Bridgeport. The experiments were also repeated in Princeton, Munich, Rome, South Africa, and Australia, with levels of obedience registering even higher than in New Haven.

14 Before the experiments began, Stanley Milgram sought predictions from a variety of people, including psychiatrists, college faculty, and graduate students. "With remarkable similarity," he wrote, "they predicted that virtually all the subjects would refuse to obey the experimenter. The psychiatrists, specifically, predicted that most subjects would not go beyond 150 volts, when the victim makes his first explicit demand to be freed. They expected that only four percent would reach 300 volts, and that only a pathological fringe of about one in a thousand would administer the highest shock on the board."

15 Why did I resist? In retrospect, I believe that my upbringing in a socialist-oriented family steeped in a class struggle view of society taught me that authorities would often have a different view of right and wrong than I would. That attitude stayed with me during my three and a half years of service in the army during World War II. Like all soldiers, I was taught to obey orders, but whenever we heard lectures on army regulations, what stayed with me was that we were also told that soldiers had a right to refuse illegal orders, though what constituted illegal was left vague.

16 In addition, in my position during the late 1940s as a staff member of the Communist Party, I had become accustomed to exercising authority and having people from a variety of backgrounds and professions carry out assignments I gave them. As a result, I had an unorthodox understanding of authority and was not likely to be impressed by a white lab coat.

17 In the early 1950s, along with other leaders of the Communist Party in Connecticut, I was arrested and tried on charges of "conspiracy to teach and advocate the overthrow of the government by force and violence." We were convicted, as expected, and I was about to go to jail when the conviction was overturned on appeal. I believe these experiences also enabled me to stand up to an authoritative "professor."

18 I was never a stereotypical "true believer" in Communist doctrine. This was one of the reasons, among others, that I left the Communist Party in the late 1950s. In any event, I believe that my political experience was an important factor in determining my skeptical behaviour in the Milgram Experiment.

19 I think the experiment had only limited relevance to our understanding of the actions of the German people under Nazi rule. In the experiment, the professor had no power to enforce his orders. In Nazi Germany, the enforcement powers went from simple reprimand all the way to imprisonment and death. In addition, the role of the learner in the experiment was markedly different from the victimized Jews, Gypsies, gay men, and others under Nazism who had not volunteered to be in an "experiment" and had no ability to stop their suffering.

20 The results of the Milgram Experiment should not surprise us. Most people unquestioningly obey orders from authorities, and refusal is unusual. As children, after all, we are taught to obey our parents, teachers, employers, and law enforcement officers. Perhaps that is why examples of refusal to obey immoral orders excite my admiration.

Vocabulary

Answer the following questions without using a dictionary. Look for context clues in the text.

1 • In Paragraph 3, what does *deceived* mean?

a) disappointed; unhappy with the outcome

(b) lied to; manipulated

c) used; not respected

2 • Find a word in Paragraph 5 or 6 that means "anxiety and concern."

suspicious

3 • What is the meaning of *demeanour* in Paragraph 9?

a) behaviour (b) appearance c) topic

4 • In Paragraph 10, what does *aroused* mean?

a) stimulated sexually

(b) aggravated or provoked

c) awakened

Comprehension

Are the following statements true or false according to the text? Circle T for "true" or F for "false." If the statement is false, write a true statement below it.

5 • Two participants randomly picked straws to determine who would be the "learner" and the "teacher." .... T (F)

One of the participant was an actor.

6 • The professor in the lab coat was actually Stanley Milgram. .... T (F)

The profesor in the lab coat was an actor.

7 • The author is no longer a member of the Communist Party. .... (T) F

He left the Communist Party in the late 50's

8 • What three things made the author suspicious that the experiment was not what it seemed to be?

- The way the straws were handled
- The idea that they would risk shocking a stranger.
- The fact that the profesor was in the area the whole time and never went watching the learner

9 • Why did the author resist authority during the experiment? Think of three reasons.

- He comes from a socialist-oriented family that teached him that autority don't have the same view

Critical Thinking

10 • Although most variations had no effect on the outcome of the experiment, Milgram tried two variations that did affect the outcome. What do these variations to the experiment tell us about human nature?

a) During the experiment, two actors resisted the professor in the lab coat and left the room. If the participant saw others resisting, he or she was more willing to resist.

This is telling us that the humans are very influencable and they don't like to be the first to do something.

b) When the participant did not touch the switch, but simply asked someone else to pull the switch, he or she was more willing to continue with the experiment.

This shows that humans feel less guilty when they act indirectly than when they act directly

11 • In Paragraph 19, Dimow says that the Milgram Experiment only has "limited relevance to our understanding of the actions of the German people under Nazi rule." Why does he say this? Restate his ideas in your own words.

Discussion

1 • In the 1960s, the majority of nurses were female. The author mentions that nurses in Bridgeport had the highest rate of compliance with authority. In your opinion, why would the compliance rate be so high among women?

2 • If the author had been one of the people who had given high voltage to the "learner," do you think he would have been so willing to write about his experiences? Why or why not?

3 • What is Dimow suggesting about soldiers who commit cruel acts?

Tip Grammar

Experience vs. *Experiment*

You have an *experience* when something happens to you. A scientist does an *experiment* in a laboratory.

The **experiment** was done with humans instead of rats.

Samuel had a life-changing **experience** in Greece when he met his future wife.

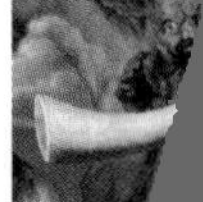

Filmmaker Alex Gibney re-examined well-known psychological tests in his documentary *The Human Behaviour Experiments*. Gibney discusses some contemporary events that reflect what happened during the Milgram and Stanford Prison experiments.

Listening Comprehension

1 • What was Milgram trying to understand?

____

2 • Why did the McDonald's assistant manager strip-search an employee?

____

3 • Why did people do what the "police officer" asked?

____

4 • How many people were called by the fake police officer? ______________

5 • Why did the young employee agree to be strip-searched?

____

____

6 • Describe Darley and Letani's experiment on group behaviour. What scenarios did they create?

____

____

____

7 • In the Darley and Letani experiment, how did people react when they were alone?

____

8 • If the subject was with other people in the room, how would he or she react?

____

9 • Gibney gives examples of real-life cases of "group think." What are two examples he discusses?

____

____

10 • What is the relevance of the experiments? What can people learn from them?

____

____

To develop your listening skills, visit the companion website.

Reading

Reading 6.2

Read about another experiment that took place in the 1970s.

The Stanford Prison Experiment

by Kathleen O'Toole

1 The view through the doorway was too familiar, like something she had seen in the international news sections of *Life* or *Newsweek*. Several young men dressed in khaki uniforms and wearing reflector sunglasses that hid their eyes were herding a larger group of men down a hallway. The latter were dressed in shapeless smocks that exposed their pale legs and the chains that bound one ankle of each man to another. Paper-bag blindfolds covered their heads.

2 Christina Maslach's stomach reacted first. She felt queasy and instinctively turned her head away. Her peers, other academic psychologists, noticed her flinch. "What's the matter?" they teased.

3 On that fateful Thursday night a quarter-century ago, Maslach would take actions that made her a heroine in some circles as "the one who stopped the Stanford Prison Experiment." Even her now-husband, Stanford psychology professor Philip Zimbardo, referred to the UC Berkeley psychologist as a hero when he spoke to a group of undergraduates in his introductory psychology class last spring. But Maslach, her professional and personal lives reshaped by that night, rejects the label.

4 Speaking at a symposium of the American Psychological Association, she urged other social science researchers to consider the circumstances of her alleged heroics. She had walked into the experiment late and therefore was more likely to be startled than those who had been planning it for months and observing it for five days, she said. She was involved in a romantic relationship with Zimbardo, the experiment's principal investigator, and not working for him as a graduate student or colleague.

5 Yet she had difficulty resisting the group pressure to be enthusiastic about what was going on in the name of science. "At that point, I felt there was something wrong with me, thinking here I am, I'm supposed to be a psychologist, I'm supposed to understand, and I was having a hard time watching what was happening to these kids."

6 In the autumn of 1971, the Stanford Prison Experiment made news in a big way. It offered the world a videotaped demonstration of how ordinary people—middle-class college students—can do things they would have never believed they were capable of doing. On Sunday morning, August 17, 1971, seventy young men, mostly college students eager to earn fifteen dollars a day for two weeks, volunteered as subjects for an experiment on prison life. After interviews and a battery of psychological tests, the two dozen judged to be the most normal, average, and healthy were selected to participate and assigned randomly either to be guards or prisoners. Those who would be prisoners were booked at a real jail, then blindfolded and driven to campus where they were led into a makeshift prison in the basement of Jordan Hall. Those assigned to be guards were given uniforms and instructed that they were not to use violence but that their job was to maintain control of the prison.

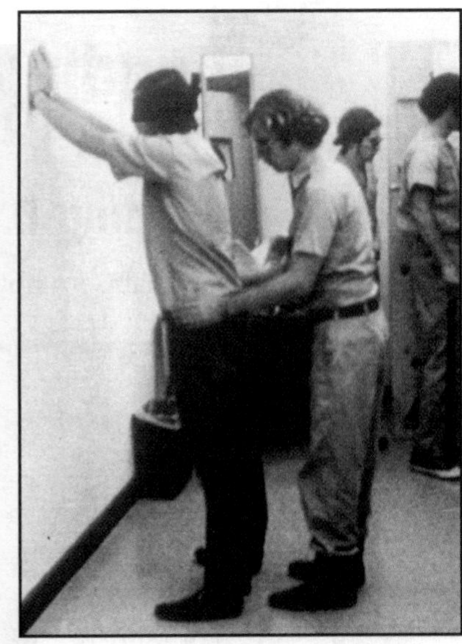

7 From the perspective of the researchers, the experiment became exciting on day two when the prisoners staged a revolt. Once the guards had crushed the rebellion, "they steadily increased their coercive aggression tactics, humiliation, and dehumanization of the prisoners," Zimbardo recalls. "The staff had to frequently remind the guards to refrain from such tactics," he said, and the worst instances of abuse occurred in the middle of the night when the guards thought the staff was not watching. The guards' treatment of the prisoners—such things as forcing them to clean out toilet bowls with their bare hands and act out degrading scenarios, or urging them to become snitches—"resulted in extreme stress reactions that forced us to release five prisoners, one a day, prematurely."

8 Zimbardo's primary reason for conducting the experiment was to focus on the power of roles, rules, symbols, group identity, and situational validation of behaviour that generally would repulse ordinary individuals. "I had been conducting research for some years that illustrated the ease with which ordinary people could be led to engage in anti-social acts by putting them in situations where they felt anonymous or they could perceive others in ways that made them less than human—as enemies or objects," Zimbardo told the Toronto symposium in the summer of 1996.

9 Maslach walked into the mock prison on the evening of the fifth day. At first, she said, she found it "dull and boring." She went to the end of the hall where some guards were waiting to start their next shift. There, she had a pleasant conversation with a "charming, funny, smart" young man waiting to start his guard shift. Other researchers had told her there was a particularly sadistic guard, whom both prisoners and other guards had nicknamed John Wayne. Later, when she looked at the monitor of the prison yard again, she asked someone to point out John Wayne and was shocked to discover it was the young man she had talked with earlier. "This man had been transformed. He was talking in a different accent, a Southern accent, which I hadn't recalled at all. He moved differently, and the way he talked was different, not just in the accent, but in the way he was interacting with the prisoners. It was like [seeing] Jekyll and Hyde. [. . .] It really took my breath away."

10 Several prisoners engaged in a debate with John Wayne, she said, in which they accused him of enjoying his job. He said that he wasn't really like that, he was just playing a role. One prisoner challenged this, Maslach said, noting that the guard had tripped him earlier when he was taking him down the hall to the bathroom. No researchers were around to see the act, the prisoner said, which indicated to him that the act reflected the guard's true disposition. John Wayne disagreed, saying that if he let up, the role wouldn't remain powerful.

11 Later that evening, Maslach said, she suddenly got sick to her stomach while watching guards taking the prisoners with paper bags over their heads to the bathroom before their bedtime. After leaving the prison with Zimbardo, she said, he asked her what she thought of it. "I think he expected some sort of great intellectual discussion about what was going on. Instead, I started to have this incredible emotional outburst. I started to scream, I started to yell, 'I think it is terrible what you are doing to those boys!' I cried. We had a

fight you wouldn't believe, and I was beginning to think, wait a minute, I don't know this guy. I really don't, and I'm getting involved with him?"

12 Zimbardo was shocked and upset by her reaction, she said, but eventually that night, "he acknowledged what I was saying and realized what had happened to him and to other people in the study. At that point he decided to call the experiment to a halt."

13 Says Zimbardo, "She challenged us to examine the madness she observed, that we had created and had to take responsibility for."

14 Maslach married Zimbardo in 1972 and became a full professor at Berkeley, studying the processes of dehumanization. In Zimbardo's view, prisons are "failed social-political experiments" that continue to bring out the worst in relations between people "because the public is indifferent to what takes place in secret there, and politicians use them, fill them up as much as they can, to demonstrate only that they are tough on crime. [. . .] They are as bad for the guards as the prisoners in terms of their destructive impact on self-esteem, sense of justice, and human compassion."

15 Craig Haney, one of Zimbardo's research associates, listed a number of lessons from the study that are largely ignored in prisons as well as in other institutions of power. The study demonstrated, for example, that "good people are not enough" to prevent abusive excess, he said. "Individual differences matter very little in the face of an extreme situation. [. . .] Institutional settings develop a life of their own independent of the wishes and intentions and purposes of those who run them."

To perfect your reading skills, visit the companion website.

Comprehension

Put your responses on a separate sheet of paper.

1 • Identify and define five difficult terms from this text.

2 • Summarize this essay. Follow the rules of summary writing found on page 55.

Watching •• The Power of the Situation

How are our beliefs and behaviour influenced by subtle situational forces? You will view excerpts from the Stanford Prison Experiment and the Moriarty Experiment.

Watching Comprehension

Are the following sentences true or false? If any statement is false, write a true statement under it.

1 • The prisoners spent 24 hours a day in the mock prison. .... T F

____

2 • The guards spent 24 hours a day in the mock prison. .... T F

____

3• Many of the prisoners developed extreme stress reactions. . . . . T F

____

4• Did any of the prisoners ask to quit the experiment? Yes No

5• How many days did the prison experiment last? ______________

6• What was Zimbardo's conclusion?

____

7• How did the experiment affect the "prisoner" who was interviewed?

____

____

8• Describe Tom Moriarty's experiment with the radio. What did he do?

____

____

____

9• During Moriarty's radio experiment, what converted people from apathy to action?

____

____

____

Discussion

In the video, Philip Zimbardo says that the Milgram and Stanford Prison experiments violated current ethical guidelines. How could the experiments have been harmful for participants?

Reading

Reading Strategy

Recognizing Irony

Irony is a technique that some writers use to make a point. When an author is being ironic, he or she says one thing but really means the opposite. There are many types of irony.

Situational irony: There is a difference between how an event looks on the surface, and what is going on underneath.

Example: A boy hears his parents whispering together. He thinks that his parents are planning a party for him. They are actually planning to divorce.

Dramatic irony: This type of irony is used in plays, stories, and novels. The audience knows something that the characters don't, which makes their actions more tragic or humorous or poignant.

Example: In Shakespeare's *Romeo and Juliet*, Romeo takes poison because he believes that Juliet is dead. The audience knows something that Romeo does not: Juliet is still alive.

Verbal irony: There is a contrast between what the writer or character says and what the writer or character means. The author uses an ironic tone and does not intend the reader to interpret the words literally. Sarcasm is a type of verbal irony.

Example: The charred burger lay in a grease-soaked bun. "That looks wonderful," he muttered.

As you read, ask yourself if the author is being serious. Perhaps the author is really being ironic in order to make a point.

Reading Exercise

Read the following selection from an essay called "The Greatest Player" by Gary Lautens.

> Occasionally I run into sports figures at cocktail parties, on the street, or on their way to the bank. "Nice game the other night," I said to an old hockey-player pal.
>
> "Think so?" he replied.
>
> "You've come a long way since I knew you as a junior."
>
> "How's that?"
>
> "Well, you high-stick better for one thing—and I think the way you clutch sweaters is really superb. You may be the best in the league."
>
> He blushed modestly. "For a time," I confessed, "I never thought you'd get the hang of it."
>
> "It wasn't easy," he confided. "It took practice and encouragement. You know something like spearing doesn't come naturally. It has to be developed."
>
> "I'm not inclined to flattery but, in my book, you've got it made. You're a dirty player," I insisted. [. . .] "There isn't a player in the league who knows as many obscene gestures. You're a gate attraction now, not just some bum who can only skate and shoot and the rest of it."

How is the selection ironic? What does the author really mean?

____

____

____

____

Reading 6.3

Italo Calvino was born in Santiago de las Vegas, Cuba, of Italian parents. As a youth, he moved with his family to Italy. During World War II, he was drafted into the Young Fascists, but he left and sought refuge in the Alps. In the following text, translated by Tim Parks, Italo Calvino brilliantly questions the whole premise behind wars. As you read, look for irony.

Conscience

by Italo Calvino

1 There came a war and a guy called Luigi asked if he could go, as a volunteer.

2 Everyone was full of praise. Luigi went to the place where they were handing out the rifles, took one and said, "Now I'm going to go and kill a guy called Alberto."

3 They asked him who Alberto was.

4 "An enemy," he answered, "an enemy of mine."

5 They explained to him that he was supposed to be killing enemies of a certain type, not whoever he felt like.

6 "So?" said Luigi. "You think I'm dumb? This Alberto is precisely that type. He is one of them. When I heard you were going to war against that lot, I thought, I'll go too, and that way I can kill Alberto. That's why I came. I know that Alberto; he's a crook. He betrayed me. For next to nothing he made me make a fool of myself with a woman. It's an old story. If you don't believe me, I'll tell you the whole thing."

7 They said fine, it was okay.

8 "Right then," said Luigi, "tell me where Alberto is and I'll go there and I'll fight."

9 They said they didn't know.

10 "Doesn't matter," Luigi said. "I'll find someone to tell me. Sooner or later I'll catch up with him."

11 They said he couldn't do that, he had to go and fight where they sent him and kill whoever happened to be there. They didn't know anything about this Alberto.

12 "You see," Luigi insisted, "I really will have to tell you the story because that guy is a real crook, and you're doing the right thing going to fight against him."

13 But the others didn't want to know.

14 Luigi couldn't see reason: "Sorry, it may be all the same to you if I kill one enemy or another, but I'd be upset if I killed someone who had nothing to do with Alberto."

15 The others lost their patience. One of them gave him a good talking to and explained what war was all about and how you couldn't go and kill the particular enemy you wanted to.

16 Luigi shrugged. "If that's how it is," he said, "you can count me out."

17 "You're in and you're staying in," they shouted.

18 "Forward march, one-two, one-two!" And they sent him off to war.

19 Luigi wasn't happy. He'd kill people, offhand, just to see if he might get Alberto or one of his family. They gave him a medal for every enemy he killed, but he wasn't happy. "If I don't kill Alberto," he thought, "I'll have killed a load of people for nothing." And he felt bad.

20 In the meantime they were giving him one medal after another, silver, gold, everything.

21 Luigi thought, "Kill some today, kill some tomorrow, there'll be less of them. That crook's bound to come."

22 But the enemy surrendered before Luigi could find Alberto. He felt bad he'd killed so many people for nothing, and since they were at peace now, he put all his medals in a bag and went around the enemy country giving them away to the wives and children of the dead.

23 Going around like this, he ran into Alberto.

24 "Good," he said, "better late than never," and he killed him.

25 That was when they arrested him, tried him for murder, and hanged him. At the trial he said over and over that he had done it to settle his conscience, but nobody listened to him.

Comprehension

Write or type your answers on a separate piece of paper. Each answer should be in a short paragraph.

1 • Why does Luigi want to kill Alberto? Explain Luigi's moral code.

2 • Explain the army's moral code. Who deserves to be killed and who doesn't?

3 • In your opinion, who is morally superior: Luigi or the other soldiers? Are any of them morally correct? Explain your answer.

4 • How is this story ironic? What is Calvino's main point? (For an explanation of irony, see the Reading Strategy on pages 78 and 79.)

5 • In your opinion, when is war justified?

Speaking •• Military Court Case

You will practise debating an issue. Imagine that you are part of a military tribunal. You must read the case below and determine whether Reservist Charles Graner is guilty of abuse. If you feel that he is guilty, decide what his punishment should be.

Your teacher will divide the class into two teams. One team must argue that Graner is innocent, and the other team must argue that he is guilty. Your team will have about ten minutes to prepare its argument. You will then have the opportunity to debate the case with the other half of the class.

The Charles Graner Case

From 2003 to 2004, Charles Graner, a thirty-five-year-old army reservist, was assigned to work in an Iraqi prison. During his time as a prison guard, he did the following:

- forced Iraqi detainees to strip and wear hoods or women's underwear on their heads;
- asked detainees to perform humiliating sexual acts while being filmed;
- hung prisoners by their hands, with their feet dangling off the floor, for hours at a time;
- punched a detainee very hard on the temple;
- hit a prisoner with a metal rod on the prisoner's open wounds;
- contributed to the death of a prisoner and was photographed smiling over the prisoner's body.

Graner was charged with gross maltreatment of detainees, assault, and failing to protect detainees. The prosecution argued that Graner was the ringleader of the prison abuse.

Graner argues that he was following orders from senior officers. He says that officers were aware of his activities and supported them. Graner testified, "I nearly beat a detainee to death while a member of military intelligence was watching."

The Suspect's Background

Graner was born in 1968. He was interested in art and drama in high school. A family friend said of Graner, "He was a really good guy. He worked hard and took good care of his kids."

Graner married in 1990. In 1991, he served a tour of duty in Saudi Arabia during the first Gulf War. He worked at a prisoner-of-war camp where there was a prison uprising. Fellow soldier Leo Bonner said that many of the reservists were profoundly changed and depressed after their experiences in Saudi Arabia.

When Graner returned home, his marriage ended and he was "devastated" according to his friends. In 1994, he worked as a guard in Fayette County prison in Pennsylvania. During his time as a guard in that prison, he was connected with several violent incidents. He was charged with putting a razor in a prisoner's potatoes, and the presiding judge said the case had "arguable merit." He was also charged with putting mace in a new guard's coffee, an incident that Graner called "a bad joke."

In 1998, Graner was charged with domestic abuse. His ex-wife accused him of yanking her out of bed by her hair and dragging her down some stairs. Criminal charges were not filed, but his ex-wife received a protection order.

The Victims

Some of the Iraqi abuse victims had not been charged with any crime. In an effort to find possible terrorists, many civilians were rounded up and brought to the prison. Although some detainees may have been involved in criminal acts, they were not all proven criminals or terrorists.

Haydar Sabbar Abed, one of the torture victims, told the British Broadcasting Corporation (BBC) he was arrested for not carrying his ID card. He said that at the prison, "They made us act like dogs, putting leashes around our necks. They'd whistle and we would have to bark like dogs. We thought they were going to kill us."

A Syrian prisoner, Ameed al-Sheikh, told the court that Graner beat him while he was recovering from a bullet wound. Al-Sheikh described Graner as the

"primary torturer" and said that Graner had forced him to perform acts that were against his beliefs, such as eating pork and drinking alcohol.

Other Testimony

Another soldier, Private Lynndie England, was also charged during the abuse scandal. She had posed in several of the photographs of abuse. Twenty-year-old England, who was dating Graner, said that Graner manipulated her. She apologized for her participation in the events.

Graner's mother says that her son is a "scapegoat" who would have been punished if he had refused to prepare the prisoners for interrogation. Staff Sergeant Ivan Frederick says that intelligence officers knew about the use of force and did not stop it. Two other soldiers in Graner's unit complained about the abuse of prisoners. The complaints were dismissed or ignored by senior officers.

Graner testified that what he did was "wrong" and that he "didn't enjoy it." He says that his orders were given by superiors, and that he was asked to prepare prisoners for interrogation: "We were asked to do certain things that I wasn't trained to do." Graner contends that he was obeying orders from military intelligence to weaken the prisoners and prepare them for interrogation.

The prosecution argues that Graner determined the type of abuse and that he appeared to enjoy punching and humiliating prisoners, as is shown in photos of him smiling over bleeding and naked detainees. The prosecution also points out that even if Graner had been following orders from senior officers, he should have known that the orders were illegal.

Is Charles Graner guilty?
If so, what should his sentence be?

Sources: CNN.com;
"Family Defends Soldier" by Dennis B. Roddy, Pittsburgh Post-Gazette;
"3 to Be Arraigned" by Christian Davenport and Michael Amon, Washington Post;
National Public Radio

Writing Topics

To review some of the vocabulary studied in this chapter, visit the companion website.

Write a composition about one of the following topics. Remember to include a thesis statement and provide supporting examples. Before handing in your work, refer to the Writing Checklist on the inside back cover.

1 • What causes wars? Think of two or three reasons why countries engage in wars.

2 • Describe a moment that changed the world. Explain some ways it has impacted people in your society.

3 • What do the Milgram Experiment and the Stanford Prison Experiment tell us about human aggression?

4 • Is killing acceptable when someone wears a military uniform? You can refer to "Conscience."

5 • When soldiers commit war crimes, is the defence of "I was following orders" legitimate? Why or why not? You might think about examples, such as when some soldiers in Iraq's Abu Ghraib prison tortured detainees.

6 • Why is history important? What can we learn from the past?

CHAPTER 7

Searching

•• You can't reason someone out of a position he didn't reason himself into. ••

Anonymous

•• The believer is happy; the doubter is wise. ••

Hungarian proverb

Throughout history, human cultures have developed belief systems, usually in the form of an organized religion, to answer life's large questions. Why are we here? What will happen after we are gone? This chapter examines spiritual beliefs.

Warm Up •• Discuss Spiritual Beliefs

Discuss the following questions with a group of students. Ensure that everybody in the group has a chance to express his or her views.

1 • Define religion. What is it?

2 • Most organized religions preach tolerance, compassion, and love, but they are often involved in persecution and violence. Why do religions clash with one another? Give examples.

3 • What features unite most of the world's major religions? List as many features as possible.

4 • Define a cult. What is the difference between a religion and a cult?

5 • Why do humans need religious beliefs?

To work on your writing skills, visit the companion website.

Tip Grammar

Believe vs. *Belief*

Believe is a verb meaning "to have faith that something is true." *Belief* is a noun meaning "a conviction."

Verb: She doesn't **believe** in ghosts.

Noun: The people of Sumatra have interesting **beliefs** about the afterlife.

Reading

Reading Strategy

Considering the Context

Each essay, story, or novel is written within a specific context. The context is the social, political, and cultural milieu in which the author lived and worked. We, as readers, may approach a reading with a completely different context. For instance, a twenty-first-century woman may feel appalled at the views about females expressed in an essay written a hundred years ago. A person who grew up in a middle-class Canadian suburb might not understand why certain traditions are followed in Nepal.

When you read essays that were written in another time or cultural milieu, be aware of the context. Question your own reactions to the reading. For example, if you feel uncomfortable with the language used or the ideas expressed, try to consider what was going on at the time and place the text was written.

Reading 7.1

In the following excerpt, Isabella Tree uses vivid detail to describe a traditional festival in Nepal. She also relates her own journey to visit the royal kumari, Nepal's official living goddess. As you read, highlight examples of effective descriptive imagery.

The Living Goddess

by Isabella Tree

Hindu goddess Durga

Dasain

1 For one week a year, Kathmandu's streets flow with the blood of a thousand animal sacrifices, and all for a vengeful, living goddess—aged only four. We arrived during Dasain, the biggest festival in the Nepali calendar, when Durga, the avenging goddess, triumphs over the forces of evil. It's a festival that celebrates the end of the monsoon and the beginning of the rice harvest. It's a time, specifically, for families—the Nepali equivalent of Christmas. Medieval, hand-powered Ferris wheels and huge bamboo swings are set up. Everyone gambles—it's the one time of the year when it's legal to do so—and even children are allowed to put down bets on board games in the street.

2 At the start of the holiday, Kathmandu is at a standstill. For eight days the streets, normally choking with traffic, are silent. It seemed we couldn't have chosen a better moment to arrive. The rains had rinsed a window in the pollution—we could even see the mountains, icing-sugar peaks, above the haze.

3 But this peacefulness was misleading. Kathmandu was not closing up shop, putting its feet up, but getting ready for the kill. While Hindus sharpened their knives, Buddhists, in implicit collusion, prayed for those who were to be given to Durga: for the goats assembling in their hundreds in Tundikhel park; for the geese and ducks massing down Kantipath; for every buffalo tethered to a stake; for every chicken in every backyard.

4 At midnight on the eighth day of Dasain, on the black night of **Kala Ratri**, the drums sounded at the shrine of Mul Chok in the ancient heart of Kathmandu, and 108 buffaloes and 108 goats had their throats slit. These represented demons that threatened the city. They were just the first of thousands to go. Early the following day, on the visitors' balcony over Kot Square, I watched another 108 beasts and 108 goats decapitated, each one with a single slice of the **kukhuri**.

5 In every household there was the twitching and kicking of a sacrifice. In the temples, people slithered up to the priest holding their offerings, their bare feet leaving skid marks on the tiles. In the streets, motorbikes and rickshaws were sprayed from the jugular of a still-bleating goat. The wheels of cars were bloodied, too, and the **bonnets** of buses. [Citizens purposely sprayed blood on vehicles in the belief that it would prevent accidents and crashes.] Kathmandu was being **purged**.

The Royal Kumari

6 A week later, Laxmi, my guide, and I were on our way to interview a living goddess—the Royal Kumari. From the moment we set foot in Kathmandu's airport, we saw the little kumari's face everywhere—on posters, postcards, and the covers of guidebooks. The origins of this extraordinary institution of the living goddess are obscure. They go back far into the mists of legend. The king of Kathmandu, they say, used to play dice with the goddess Taleju. One day, the king made an improper advance, and the goddess was so angered that she threatened to withdraw her protection of the Kathmandu Valley. The king begged her to stay, and at last she relented. But to put herself beyond temptation's reach, she agreed to return only in the body of a prepubescent girl. Whatever the origins, the kumari is the life and soul of Kathmandu. "Without her," Laxmi said, "our city is lost."

7 A kumari's life is necessarily bizarre. From the age of two or three she is closeted in secret chambers in a palace in the ancient heart of the city. She sees nobody but her priests and caretakers. Her parents may visit, but must kneel at her feet. Most of her day is spent in ritual and prayer. But as soon as she bleeds, be it a graze or a cut, or inevitably, puberty, the goddess leaves her and hovers about, insubstantial for a while until another suitable host can be found.

8 To this day, the king of Kathmandu bows to the sovereignty of the royal kumari. It is the little girl who crowns the king; it is she who receives him kneeling at her throne every year for her blessing; and in times of crisis—drought, famine, plague—the king begs her forgiveness and appeals to her to put things right.

9 In the old part of town beyond Durbar Square, I steeled myself to confront the goddess and stepped into the courtyard of the Kumari Bahal. I waited with a group of French tourists while an attendant counted his **baksheesh** and then called up to a window framed in gold leaf, on the third floor.

•• **Kala Ratri** A destructive goddess from Hindu mythology. On the night of Kala Ratri, animals are sacrificed to celebrate victory over evil.
•• **kukhuri** sacrificial knife
•• **bonnet** British word for the hood that covers the car engine
•• **purged** cleansed
•• **baksheesh** bribe

 Royal Kumari

10 "Hey, Goddess!" Moments later there was a flicker of movement behind the shutters and the goddess appeared. She could only have been four or five years old, but she was made up like a woman on a good night out. Her eyes were black with kohl, her lips were red, her clothes red, her hair piled up under the famous peacock crown, and she was dripping with jewels.

11 She looked down on us mere mortals for a few dutiful moments before turning back to her devotions. That split second was revelatory. She looked at us with petulance: bored, **sulky**, yet fiery and defiant. Here was no symbol of charity or innocence. Here was a creature with the heart of a tigress. That she was a child was almost an irrelevance. Her virginity is what gave her power: the unambiguous awesome power of a woman untamed by man. This was why she dressed in reds, the colour of married women, and not the whites and yellows of purity.

Choosing a Living Goddess

12 More than ever, I was intrigued to know more about her. What was it like to be taken away from home at the age of two, isolated, and worshipped? An audience with the kumari was, for a foreigner, strictly forbidden. But Laxmi knew someone who could arrange an interview with the kumari who had reigned before this one. Was I interested?

13 The girl we were about to meet was now fifteen. Like all the royal kumaris before her, she would have been born into the elite Buddhist Sakya caste, and she had passed a strict selection process.

14 When a potential goddess is a small child, her parents put her name forward to a special committee consisting of five Buddhist priests, a Brahman priest, and the royal astrologer. Along with several other candidates—all between the ages of two and four—she is subjected to an ancient process of elimination. The committee scrutinizes each girl for thirty-two physical perfections, the most obvious being that she is in perfect health, has black hair and eyes, and no blemishes or bad body smells. The other aspects they look for are disconcertingly Lolitaesque. The kumari must have thighs like those of a deer, for example, a neck like a conch shell, a tongue that is small and sensitive, a voice as clear and soft as a duck's, eyelashes like those of a cow, and hands that are soft and firm.

15 The ultimate test is carried out a few weeks later as final proof that the goddess has possessed one particular child. On the eighth day of Dasain, the little kumari-elect is led to the inner courtyard of the shrine of Mul Chok. Inside, the 108 buffalo heads are laid out in rows. In the shadows, men would lurk with the faces of demons. The child must walk clockwise round the courtyard, in complete composure. Finally, if she does not betray a flicker of fear, the priests lead her to an upper storey in the palace to worship her as the deity.

16 I wasn't sure what a royal kumari would be like, even three years after the goddess had left her. With all the traumas of severed heads and demons, the orphaned isolation, kingly indulgence and priestly repression, the image wasn't promising. Added to that was what had happened to her since that moment of her own natural bloodshed. After her dethronement,

•• **sulky** unhappy

she returned, without jewels, a crown, or makeup, to a family she no longer knew and to the horrors of insignificance.

Meeting a Former Goddess

17 Laxmi stopped at a door in a tiny courtyard. We were invited in by her father, and after ten minutes of chat, the former royal kumari slipped into the room and took up her place on a sofa at the far end. Her shyness and beauty were intoxicating. She averted her eyes from us most of this time, gazing instead at the fingers twisting in her lap. But occasionally, when she heard Laxmi translating my questions, she would flash us a glance and a smile of such brilliance that it made one want to weep.

18 Scarcely had she entered, however, than her two elder sisters stormed the place. They were pretty but big and pushy. They were thrilled to find an audience for their English, and intercepted my questions with lightening reflexes. They told me about the selection process; how they used to visit the kumari; how they would bow and call her "God-sister"; how she would play with her dolls and, occasionally, the caretaker's children; how she was made up and dressed every day; of the queues of people waiting to see her. All the while my blood boiled with frustration as I tried again and again to fire words past their defences.

19 Eventually, after half an hour, they left. I thought the former kumari would feel free to talk, but I was wrong. The sisters had been playing a part that had evolved out of necessity. The more I tried to coax my subject to speak, the less she seemed able to do so. My questions were like chains that threatened to choke her. She would utter a word, a single tiny sound that I strained to catch; then her parents would expand it into an answer.

20 Yes—the kumari suggested—she had wanted to play outside, to run and skip with other children, but she was a goddess, so naturally she couldn't. Of course she wasn't frightened by all the blood on Kala Ratri. Yes, she had felt different as the kumari.

21 Her answers about present life were a little more direct. The hardest thing, she indicated, was negotiating the people and traffic in the streets. Until then, she had only walked the length of her chamber. On the few occasions she had shown herself outside, such as on festival days, she had been carried by chariot. Life as a mortal was, literally, about finding one's feet.

22 She was at school now and having a hard time of it. As a goddess, she had received schooling from her caretaker, but it hadn't prepared her for ninth grade. She felt distant from the rest of her class. The principal still addressed her first, in **deference** to her past. She felt happier at home now, though she had felt angry and awkward at first.

23 What of the future? Would she ever like to marry and have children? She smiled a **bashful** yet sorrowful smile. Her parents didn't bother to expand. The likelihood of finding a man brave enough to marry her was remote. Most Nepalese men believe this would be the kiss of death; they would die horribly on the wedding night if they married a former kumari. Even men who were educated, worldly, and less prone to superstition would be reluctant to take on a woman who might demand to be treated like a goddess—who wasn't used to doing the shopping.

24 When the interview ended, most of the questions I had written down in my notebook had been crossed off unanswered. Yet the meeting had been mysteriously inspiring. This

•• **deference** respect

•• **bashful** shy or timid

lovely, lonely creature had moved me in a way that made a mockery of my journalistic interrogations. The emptiness at her core—that absent distraction, that serene ethereal gaze—was how I imagined a person to look at the moment of death, like an empty beautiful shell. It had been pointless—I saw that now—to try to learn about her time as a goddess. But I came away at least with an idea of what it was for her to be one no longer.

25 When we got outside, the world was a sordid place. A couple of crackheads tried to beg money off us. Dogs fornicated on a garbage dump. Someone was defecating in the gutter. And back on the fume-filled roads, the traffic jerked and blared, though it was almost eight o'clock. A low-pressure smog had descended on the city. Somewhere beyond the cacophony, in the quiet Durbar Square, it was comforting to remember that another little girl was perched on her throne, ready to do battle for Kathmandu.

Vocabulary

1 • What is the meaning of *tethered* in Paragraph 3? ______________

2 • Find a word in Paragraph 17 that means "looking intently." ______________

3 • Find a word in Paragraph 19 that means "persuade." ______________

4 • Find a word in Paragraph 23 that means "unhappy." ______________

Comprehension

5 • Why do people slaughter animals during the Dasain festival?

____

6 • What is the royal kumari?

____

____

7 • Briefly sum up some tests a girl must pass before being declared a kumari.

____

____

____

8 • Describe how a kumari lives.

____

____

9 • The author has a chance to meet a former kumari. How old is the girl? ________

10 • Describe the former kumari's character.

____

____

11 • What are some disadvantages of being a kumari?

___

___

___

___

___

12 • What is the author suggesting in her concluding paragraph? Why does Kathmandu need a royal kumari?

___

___

___

Discussion

To practise your speaking skills, visit the companion website.

The kumari is isolated from the general public, and treated as a special, superior being. Is there any equivalent in your culture?

Reading Strategy

Identifying Figurative Devices

Some writers use figurative devices such as similes or metaphors to make their writing more descriptive. A **simile** is a comparison using *like* or *as*.

She drops names like autumn trees drop leaves.

A **metaphor** is a comparison that does not use *like* or *as*.

The drunk's legs were rubber.

Writers can also use **personification**, which is the act of attributing human qualities to an inanimate object, idea, or animal.

The wind kicked the leaves.

Her recollections cut away the years.

Imagery is description using the five senses: sight, hearing, taste, touch, and smell. Look at the following examples of imagery.

Sight: "When I put my foot down in the powder, the boot print preserved itself exquisitely."

From "What It Feels Like to Walk on the Moon" by Buzz Aldrin

Hearing: "Paul heard the clicking of the woman's heels across the floor."

From "Next Door" by Kurt Vonnegut Jr.

Touch: The starched collar of the white shirt rubbed against my neck.

Smell: "The car's interior emanated a distinct aroma of wet tennis shoes and old carpet."

From "The Wake Up Call" by Jennifer Alvira

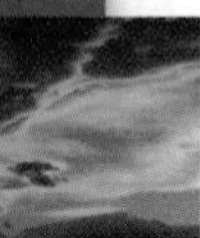

To perfect your reading skills, visit the companion website.

Reading Exercise

To answer the following questions, look in "The Living Goddess."

1 • Underline a metaphor in Paragraph 2.

2 • Underline two examples of personification in Paragraphs 2 and 3.

3 • Underline examples of simile in Paragraphs 10 and 14.

4 • In the concluding paragraph, highlight at least three vivid images that appeal to the senses. (Think about images that appeal to one of the following: seeing, hearing, touch, taste, or smell.)

Speaking •• Describe It

Your teacher will divide the class into two large teams. Each team will be made up of pairs of students.

With your partner, write the names of five objects on a piece of paper. Try to be creative in your choice of object. (The object can be an animal, a vegetable, a mineral, a plastic or metal object, etc.)

When you have finished making your list, hand in your sheet. Your teacher will redistribute your team's sheets to the other group of students. You will receive a paper that someone on the other team wrote. You and your partner must stand in front of your group and describe, one by one, the objects on your sheet without using the actual words. For example, if the object is a garbage can, you cannot use either word—*garbage* or *can*—to describe it. Instead, you should appeal to your audience by using clues, or words that refer to various aspects of the object in question—for example, its function, shape, colour, texture, odour, taste, or a noise it might make, etc.

Watching •• The Pursuit of Happiness

Scientists and Tibetan Buddhist monks have collaborated on a project that uses meditation to treat mood disorders. Watch the video and then answer the following questions.

Watching Comprehension

1 • Where is the Dalai Lama's residence, the town of Dharamsala, located?

a) Tibet **b)** India **c)** China

Are the following statements true or false? If you think a statement is false, write a true statement under it.

2 • Richard Davidson is a brain researcher at the University of Nebraska.... T F

____

3 • Davidson received a research grant of fifteen million dollars............. T F

____

4 • People become much happier after winning a lottery....................... T F

____

5 • Everyone's emotional set point of happiness is impossible to change...... T F

____

6 • Which part of the brain is active during times of fear and anxiety?

a) left side of the front cortex **b)** right side of the front cortex

7 • Which part of the brain is active during feelings of joy and contentment?

a) left side of the front cortex **b)** right side of the front cortex

8 • How do monks' brains differ from average brains, according to brain imaging tests?

____

____

Discussion

1 • Tibetan monks must spend at least 10,000 hours, which represents many years, meditating and practising other forms of mental training. They must also remove themselves from temptations and the emotional roller-coaster that most people live on, which includes love, heartbreak, work stresses, child-raising, and so on. Is the trade-off worth it? Why or why not?

2 • What does the video suggest about the lives of people in Western countries? How can people in the West become more resilient and content?

Reading

Reading 7.2

The following short story looks at the theory of predestination, which is the belief that every detail of our lives is preordained. Award-winning Canadian author Hugh Garner raises some intriguing questions on the subject of fate.

The Premeditated Death of Samuel Glover

by Hugh Garner

1 It's been nothing but questions all day at the office. Every few minutes one of the other draftsmen would come over to my board and ask me about Sam's death. "What happened

last night? Were you with him? Did it knock him down? Run over him? How did he look? Was there much blood?"

2 They have no idea what it's like seeing a friend get killed like that and having to answer all the questions by the police, the taxi company lawyer, and then by the fellows at work the next day. I'm going to tell it once more, the whole thing, and then I'm through.

3 Every night at five o'clock for the last seven or eight years Sam Glover and I had taken the elevator together, going home. Sam would buy his evening paper in the lobby, and then we'd walk up the street as far as Queen where we separated, Sam to take a westbound streetcar, and me to take one going east.

4 It got to be a habit, this three-block walk, and I enjoyed it because Sam was an interesting old fellow to talk to. He was a bachelor who lived with a married sister way out in the west end of town. From some of the things he told me on these short walks, I learned that he was a believer in things like fate and predestination. It was his favourite subject, and sometimes he'd point to people who passed us on the street and say, "There goes a man hurrying to his fate," or "He wants to reach his rendezvous, that one."

5 I'd laugh, and he'd say, "You'll find out some day that it's no joke. I've seen it happen. Every man is predestined to meet his death at a time and place already chosen, my boy."

6 I'd laugh and shake my head.

7 It was about three years ago that Sam told me where he was going to die. We were waiting for the lights to change at the intersection of Adelaide Street, when Sam said, "This is the place where fate is going to catch up to me."

8 I looked down at him and laughed, thinking he was joking. He was the type of mousy little guy who would joke like that—or dismember a corpse.

9 "You may laugh, son, but it's true," he asserted in the good-natured, yet serious, way he had.

10 "Do you mean to tell me that you're going to be killed on this corner?" I asked.

11 "That's right," he answered soberly.

12 When the lights changed, we crossed the street. I said to Sam, "If you know that you're going to be killed here, why do you take this way home? You could walk a block east or west and take the streetcar from there."

13 "It wouldn't be much use trying to avoid it," he answered. "Some day I'd forget, or have some business to transact down here."

14 "Well, suppose you decided not to die at all. You could move to another town and live forever."

15 "Nobody lives forever," he answered patiently. "You can't avoid your fate. This is where it will happen, and nothing I can do will prevent it. I'm just hoping that it won't be for some time yet." He looked up at me and smiled apologetically, but I could see that he meant every word.

16 After that, I brought the subject up occasionally as we were crossing Adelaide Street, kidding him about being shortsighted and about getting killed before his time if he wasn't careful. He would only smile at me and say, "You wait and see."

17 Last night, we left the office as usual, about two minutes to five, in order to beat the rush to the elevators. Sam bought his paper in the lobby, and we went out into the street.

18 As we brushed through the five-o'clock crowd, I asked Sam how his dike drawings for the Mountview Refinery were coming along, and he told me he expected to finish them in a week. He was only waiting for some new tank specifications from McGuire, one of the engineers.

19 Looking up into the blue sky above the buildings, I said, "It's going to be a nice evening. A change from the rain we've been having."

20 "Yes, it is. I'm going to do a little lawn bowling tonight," he answered. "It'll be my first chance this year. The greens have been a mess up to now."

21 When we reached the corner of Adelaide, the lights were in our favour, and we began to cross with the crowd. They changed from green to amber when we were halfway across, but we still had plenty of time. He stuck close to me as he always did. I saw this taxi cut around the traffic and begin to cross the intersection as soon as it got the green light, so I shouted to Sam and ran the last few yards to the sidewalk.

22 I looked around and saw the taxi pick him up and throw him with a sickening plop against a hydrant about twenty feet from the corner. There was the scream of the taxi's brakes and a lot of yelling from the crowd.

23 By the time I got there, two men had laid Sam out on the sidewalk. Everybody was crowding around to get a better look at him. He was dead, of course. One side of his head was squashed like the soft spot of an orange.

24 A policeman butted his way through the crowd and asked what had happened. The hack driver came over from his car and told the policeman that he hadn't had a chance, this old man ran right in front of his cab. He seemed to be a nice young fellow, and he wanted us all to believe him. I told the policeman I was a friend of Sam's, and that I had seen the accident. I assured the driver that it wasn't his fault.

25 The taxi company lawyer came to my place later in the evening and questioned me about the accident. "I can't understand why he'd turn around and run the other way," he kept on saying.

26 " I've told you it wasn't your driver's fault, so why do you keep asking me questions like that?"

27 "Okay. I'm only trying to **dope this thing out** in case they have an inquest," he said.

28 If they have an inquest, I'm going to tell the truth. I've been thinking it over, and I feel sure that Sam would have wanted it that way.

29 I had nothing against the old fellow, but after listening for so long to him bragging about knowing where he was going to die, it seemed I had to find out whether he was right or not. When I shouted at him to turn back, it wasn't me talking at all. Call it fate or predestination, or what you like, but that's what killed Sam Glover.

•• **dope this thing out** understand

Comprehension

1 • Describe the relationship between Sam and the narrator.

____

____

2 • When Sam and the narrator were crossing the intersection at the time of the accident, what colour was the light when they began crossing?

____

3 • When the narrator saw the cab coming, in which direction did he run?

____

4 • As the cab came toward the two men, what did the narrator shout to Sam?

____

5 • Why did the narrator shout those words? _______________

____

6 • In Paragraph 8, the narrator says, "He was the type of mousy little guy who would joke like that—or dismember a corpse." What does this sentence tell you about the narrator's feelings toward Sam?

____

____

7 • Does the narrator believe in predestination? Support your answer.

____

____

____

8 • Who is responsible for Sam's death?

____

____

____

Discussion / Written Response

1 • Who or what is responsible for Sam's death?

2 • Discuss the significance of the title, "The Premeditated Death of Samuel Glover." Think about the meaning of the word *premeditated*.

3 • If it were true that everyone is predestined to meet his or her death at a time and place already chosen, would you want to know when, where, or how you will die? Why or why not?

Listening •• Mother of a Cult Leader

In Hinduism, a guru is a teacher or guide. In English, the word has come to mean a spiritual leader. Luna Tarlo's son, Andrew Cohen, developed a cult and acts as the cult's guru. For a brief period, Luna became involved in her son's organization and she documented her experiences in her book *Mother of God*. Listen to the interview and answer the following questions.

Luna Tarlo and her son Andrew

Listening Comprehension

1 • How did Andrew Cohen become a guru? Briefly describe what led to his "enlightenment."

____

____

____

2 • What did Luna discover about her son when she arrived in India?

____

____

3 • When did Andrew begin his organization? ____________________

4 • What types of people join cults?

____

____

5 • According to Luna, why do people go to gurus?

____

____

6 • How did Andrew's organization grow?

____

____

7 • What is Andrew's cult like? Describe it.

____

____

____

8 • What is Andrew's main philosophy?

____

____

9 • Luna now calls her son a "monster." What are some examples of Andrew's cruelty?

____

____

____

10 • Why did Luna remain a part of Andrew's organization for several years? You will have to make a guess.

____

____

____

Discussion

Why are there so many cults in North America? What are people searching for? Why do they go to cults instead of traditional organized religions?

A battle is raging in Kansas about the teaching of evolution. Visit the companion website to view a television segment about religion and politics.

Writing Topics

Write a composition about one of the following topics. Remember to include a thesis statement and provide supporting examples. Before handing in your work, refer to the Writing Checklist on the inside back cover.

1 • Explain why all societies have particular festivals and celebrations. What are the benefits of such celebrations?

2 • Thomas Wolfe once said, "A cult is a religion with no political power." Define a cult. Explain how is a cult different from other organized religions. You can give examples from the audio interview with Luna Tarlo.

To review some of the vocabulary studied in this chapter, visit the companion website.

3 • Should religion or moral education have a role in schools? Why or why not? Back up your views with specific examples and anecdotes.

4 • Respond to "The Premeditated Death of Samuel Glover." What is the message or theme of the essay? (For tips on responding to short stories, see Writing Workshop 5).

5 • Why do people believe in gods and spirits? You might support your views with examples from the readings in this chapter.

CHAPTER 8

Ethics

•• *One's first step in wisdom is to question everything—and one's last is to come to terms with everything.* ••

Georg Christoph Lichtenberg

Throughout our lives, we are confronted with situations that test our values. In this chapter, you will read about ethical dilemmas.

Warm Up •• Preparing Arguments

When you write essays or do oral presentations, you are asked to present your thesis and supporting arguments. This activity offers you the opportunity to practise developing thesis statements and supporting arguments.

Work with a partner or a small group of students. Choose one of the cases listed below and then do the following:

- Read about the issue and discuss the questions.
- Create a thesis statement and come up with three supporting ideas.

Case A: Social Host Responsibility

Ottawa citizens Dwight Courrier and Julie Zimmerman had a BYOB (bring your own booze) New Year's party. One of their guests, alcoholic Desmond Desormeaux, had about twelve beers. He sat in the basement and drank by himself. Then he drove home. He had a head-on collision with a car containing five young people. One passenger was killed, and another, Zoe Childs, was left a paraplegic. Childs sued the social hosts, arguing that they should be responsible for their drunken party guests.

- Should social hosts be held legally responsible for their drunken guests?
- For the last thirty years, commercial drinking establishments have been legally responsible for their drunken customers. How is a bartender different from a social host?
- What punishment should drunk drivers receive?

Case B: Parenthood and Age

In Turkey, after thirty-five years of trying, sixty-four-year-old Memnune Tiryaki became pregnant. Adriana Emilia Iliescu, a Romanian woman, was sixty-seven years old when she gave birth to her daughter Eliza. And a Spanish woman was sixty-seven when she gave birth to twins. All three women received in vitro fertilization—using donors' eggs.

Comedian Charlie Chaplin had his youngest son when he was seventy-two. One of the world's oldest fathers is Les Colley, who became a father at ninety-two, after marrying his Fijian bride whom he met through a dating agency.

- Should there be a legal age limit for parenthood?
- If there is an age limit for women, should there also be one for men?
- What are some advantages and disadvantages of being an older parent?

Case C: Soccer Coach

Jim Ferris is a soccer coach for a high level AAA team. The team has a chance to play nationally. The players are twelve to fourteen years of age. Ferris has pressure from his soccer association to win games. On the other hand, some of his weakest players are very motivated and excited, and he would like to give them time on the field. If he plays his weak players, he will lose more games. When he doesn't play those players, their parents yell and complain, and the children are disappointed.

- Should coaches of children's teams always give equal field time to weak players?
- Should parents be banned from games if they object to the coaching?
- What should the goal of soccer associations be?

To practise your speaking skills, visit the companion website.

Thesis Statement and Supporting Ideas

Write your thesis statement and supporting ideas here.

Thesis statement: ______________________________

Supporting arguments:

1 • ______________________________

____

2 • ______________________________

____

3 • ______________________________

____

Reading

Reading 8.1

Alicia Gifford is a Los Angeles-based writer and editor, and her work appears in a number of online and print journals, as well as in several short fiction anthologies. She is the fiction editor for the literary journal *Night Train*. In the following short story, the main character deals with a very difficult dilemma.

Toggling the Switch

by Alicia Gifford

1 On Tuesday, Toni meets her lover, Gordon, for dinner downtown at the Water Grill. They each have a martini at the bar while they wait for a table. They get seated and both order salads. She orders blackened salmon, and he orders Maine lobster. They get a bottle of Chardonnay.

2 They make small talk while they eat their salads. He's fidgety and distracted. She drinks her wine and wonders what his problem is.

3 The assistant waiter clears the salad plates, and then the headwaiter sets down their main courses while the assistants scuttle around pouring more water and more wine.

4 "What's up?" Toni asks when the waiter leaves. She cuts a piece of salmon and holds the steaming fish in the air on the tines of her fork. He looks at her.

5 "Elaine's pregnant," he says. Elaine is Gordon's wife.

6 Toni puts the fish in her mouth and chews slowly, sucking in air because it's still too hot. She stares at him while he slices his lobster, beautifully laid out on a bed of linguine. With her mouth full she says, "*Really*? And you're the lucky daddy?"

7 He reddens. "We shared a bottle of champagne followed by cognac a few weeks ago, our anniversary. That's the first time we've had sex in months." He takes a bite of lobster, chews and swallows, and says, "She wants the baby. She wants to get counselling. She knows I've been having an affair."

8 Toni picks up the glass of Chardonnay and takes three large gulps, then wipes her mouth with her hand. The chilled wine tastes good. This is fine, she tells herself. This is a good thing. She's on overtime with this dead-end trip. She's been insane to carry on with him anyway. If the stuffy financial advisement firm she works for found out she's been having an affair with a client—a *married* client—she'd be fired. Still—

9 "I'm really very fond of you," he says, staring at his plate. "But I told her I'd try. I told her I'd go to counselling, that I'd work on the marriage."

10 "You should," she says. "I never intended for this to go on this long anyway. I'm *glad* she's pregnant," she says. "Congratulations. No, really," she says, swallowing. "It's fine. I was going to tell you it was over tonight anyway." Which is almost true. She was planning to break up the last three or four times they were together; it's just that she too is fond of him.

11 The wine gives her a great buzz. She feels reckless and dramatic.

12 "I'll miss you," she says. She raises her glass in a toast. "Here's to great fun—just one of those things." She empties her glass and stands up, wanting to get out before she gets mawkish and sloppy. She picks up her purse and hardly staggers when she walks away, slowly, swaying her hips with deliberate sensuality.

13 *Just one of those things*, Toni sings out loud, walking out of the restaurant, *just one of those crazy things*. It's June but the evening is cool. A few tears well in her eyes, and she enjoys the self-pity. She's exhilaratingly drunk. She calls her friend Lenny and asks if he's busy. He's a TV producer between jobs, spending his time playing video games and getting high. He also sells pot now and then, when his source in northern California has some to unload, to make lots of extra cash. Lenny's ten years younger, and at one time

they'd toyed with romantic notions and sexual attraction but decided there would be more longevity to their relationship if they remained friends. "Well, yeah, I'm busy," he says. "I'm kicking Nazi butt. Come over."

14 She drives to his apartment in Santa Monica in her 4Runner. She'd left her BMW Z3 Roadster at home tonight, and she's glad. She feels safer hurtling on the freeway with the bulk of her SUV around her. She puts on Diana Krall and belts the bluesy jazz in her off-key contralto on the Santa Monica Freeway. She's going to miss Gordon—his charm, intelligence, the fantastic sex—but she knows herself well enough to realize that much of his appeal came from the *verboten* nature of their relationship.

15 When she gets to Lenny's, he offers her a beer and a bong hit while he finishes playing a round of *Return to Castle Wolfenstein*. "Take *that*," he says, and shuts down the game. "So what happened with Mr. Party-in-his-Pants?" he asks. She tells him.

16 "Loser," he says. "Life 101: No affairs with married men."

17 "Yeah, well." He's right, of course. Affairs with married men were as feckless as her former indulgence in sweaty, one-night trysts with college boys. At least she'd stopped that. She didn't know why she had to **toggle** her self-destruct switch to feel alive.

18 She's not hungry but eats some of his cold pizza anyway and drinks a beer. They do a couple shots of tequila. They watch *Blade Runner* on Lenny's home theatre system and pass the bong. She dozes for a half hour on the sofa, her head propped on her hand.

19 "I'm going to bed," Lenny says abruptly. "Crash on the sofa."

20 "I've got to get home," she says rubbing her neck.

21 "You can't drive."

22 "I'm fine. I've got to work in the morning," she says, but Lenny's already nodded off in his cushy leather recliner that does everything but his laundry.

23 She gets in her car, stops at a donut shop to get coffee and an apple fritter. She drives with the windows down and lets the cold air smack her face. She gets on the 405 heading north but gets off at Ventura Boulevard because she's weaving. She blasts a Pearl Jam CD as she carefully drives the empty streets heading east across the Valley toward Burbank, coming to complete stops and minding the speed limit. She feels wired, hopeful. She wants to meet someone and have a relationship, something healthy and decent. The breakup is an opportunity, a good thing. Decency, that's what she needs in her life.

24 The moon is out. It's nearly one in the morning when she gets to her neighbourhood. The streets are deserted, the houses dark. Only the coyotes are active, darting in the shadows.

25 She heads up the narrow canyon to her house, looking forward to her bed, when ahead of her a kid shoots down a steep driveway on a skateboard, straight at her. A split second in her headlights—wide blue eyes, a blur of freckles, Spiderman pyjamas—then the thick thud of impact—and he disappears.

26 She throws the car into park and gets out. He's in the gutter, head against the curb. In the amber streetlight she sees blood coming from his ears and mouth. His eyes are half-open, dead. Dark, wet tissue—with hair—hangs off the concrete.

27 She shakes violently. She squats, checks for a pulse with her fingers on his neck—his head rolls—a ghastly angle—and blood and brain leak out. She gets her cellphone—no service

•• **toggle** snap or turn on or off

in this part of the canyon. She runs up to the house that he came from and rings the bell and pounds the door, but no one's there.

28 She goes back to where he's lying and tugs his pyjama top down to cover his belly. "Oh honey, I'm so sorry, so sorry," she says, her face slimy with tears and mucus. She staggers to her car, gets in, and shifts into gear. She pulls away, slowly at first, and then faster, not looking back.

29 She'll call from her house. She'll call the police and explain everything, how he came from nowhere, how she tried to report it.

30 Inside her garage, she shuts the door. She looks at the car; the boy's body has left a slight impression on the grill. She's wide awake—but drunk. She can taste and smell alcohol. She's stoned on pot. What's going to happen if she calls to report a hit-and-run?

31 He's dead. Nothing can help him. It wasn't her fault. A sober person would've hit him.

32 She'll hold off calling until the alcohol clears her system. She sits, staring, seeing the boy, the broken egg of his head.

33 She dozes, and now it's dawn. She calls her office and leaves a message that she's sick. She turns on the TV. Around eight she hears it on the Channel 4 News. "A hit-and-run has claimed the life of nine-year-old Freddie Lasko in Burbank while he was apparently out skateboarding." The boy's parents were out of town attending a funeral. The boy's sister found him around three when she came home. The phone number of the Burbank police flashes on the screen.

34 She should call a lawyer, but only tax and corporate attorneys come to mind. She needs a criminal lawyer—*Christ.* She covers her mouth with her hands. She can't make decisions right now; she needs to clear her mind, to rest. She takes a sleeping pill and turns off the phone.

35 She wakes up at four in the afternoon, disoriented. The memories start to download, and she runs to the bathroom to vomit.

36 She turns on her phone and the news.

37 "Still no clue as to who killed Freddie Lasko some time this morning while he rode his skateboard," a reporter says, standing outside the family home. "Police need your help ..."

38 The phone rings. "Hey, it's Lenny. 'Sup? I called your office and they said you were sick."

39 "Oh God, Lenny. Something's happened. Something awful." Sobbing, she tells him about the accident.

40 "Call a lawyer and turn yourself in," he says.

41 "I'll lose my job. I'm up to become a partner."

42 "You killed a kid."

43 "He was skateboarding at one in the morning. His parents left him with a flaky sister. If anything, *they're* negligent."

44 "I told you not to drive."

45 "He came from nowhere, down a driveway, like a shot."

46 "Tell them you were with me. Tell them we played Scrabble, drank tea. You drove home, killed him, and panicked. They don't have to know you were drinking. Get a lawyer."

47 "Look, I'll talk to you later," she says.

48 She slips on some sweatpants, a T-shirt, and her walking shoes. She gets her Walkman and tunes in the news. She walks down to the boy's street. She gets near the house, strolling with deliberate nonchalance, a decent woman out for an afternoon walk. Police are there; the area around the curb is taped off. A media truck is parked on the street. Toni walks to where a detective stands under a tree, smoking a cigarette.

49 "I heard about this on the news," she says. "Any progress?"

50 The detective looks at her, blows smoke through his nostrils, then crushes the cigarette under his foot. He picks up the butt, puts it into a baggie, and pockets it.

51 "You live around here?" he asks.

52 "A few blocks away."

53 "Housewife?" he asks.

54 "Uh, no." She smiles at him, but he doesn't smile back. She regrets talking to him—what was she thinking? She's the proverbial perp, returning to the scene of the crime.

55 "Not much to go by. Probably someone local," he says. "Whereabouts did you say you live?"

56 She tells him the wrong street.

57 "Humour me. Where were you between midnight and three in the morning?"

58 "Me?"

59 "Just doing my job, ma'am," he says. "Where were you last night? Do you mind?"

60 "I spent the night in Santa Monica. I was with my friend."

61 He reaches into his pocket, pulls out his card, gives it to her. "If you hear anything."

62 She takes the card, and he pulls out a notebook. "What kind of a car do you drive, anyway?" he asks.

63 "I kind of resent this," she says, mustering indignation.

64 "You got something to hide?"

65 "I drive a BMW Z3," she says.

66 "Bet you look good in it, too," he says. Now he smiles. "Anyone at your place drive an SUV?"

67 "No."

68 "Know anyone in the neighbourhood with an SUV?"

69 "Maybe fifty percent, around here," she says.

70 He laughs. "Yeah, that's about right," he says. "Why don't you give me your name and address, phone number too. That way we'll know we already talked to you."

71 She makes it all up.

72 "Have a nice day," he says, touching his finger to his forehead. He puts the notebook away and pulls out another cigarette.

73 She starts to walk away when a woman approaches her from one of the houses. "He gave me the third degree too," she says. "I live across from the Laskos. I almost killed Freddy

twice—see? Those are my skid marks right there." She points to the black tire marks in the street. "That kid loved to come streaking down that driveway. I told his parents he'd get killed."

74 "It happened at night, right?"

75 "His folks were in Sacramento. Jody—that's Freddy's sister—was out on a date or something when it happened." The woman shakes her head. "How anyone could leave a dead kid like that is beyond me."

76 "Horrible," Toni croaks. She's light-headed, nauseated. She breaks into a cold sweat.

77 The woman leans in, drops her voice. "I heard the coyotes got to him. I heard his head was nearly *gone*—can you imagine? That poor doll finding her brother like that?"

78 "*God.*" Toni covers her mouth. Spasms jerk her throat. She sees the detective eyeballing them as they talk.

79 "Losing a kid's gotta be the worst," the woman says, shaking her head. She looks at her watch. "Nice talking to you." She hands Toni a business card. "Think of me for all your real estate needs."

80 Toni gets back to her house, and there's a message from Lenny on her voice mail. *"Hey, give me a call."*

81 The phone rings. It's Gordon. "I—I need to talk to you," he says. "Elaine's not pregnant. She made it up. I told her I want a divorce."

82 Why is he calling? It's like the information is stored in some archive in her brain she can't access.

83 He says, "Did you hear me? I'm leaving Elaine. I love you."

84 She lets out a shrill laugh.

85 "*Jesus,*" he says, "I don't see what's funny."

86 "You love me? It's *hilarious.*" She hangs up. He repulses her. She gags up a bilious mini-vomit and swallows it.

87 In the garage she inspects the 4Runner again, moving her fingers over the slight dent in the polished chrome. She sees herself reflected in the curve of it, her head tiny and distant, her feet clownish and huge.

88 The phone rings. It's Lenny. "Have you done anything?" he asks.

89 "Uh-uh." She swallows. "It wasn't my fault. I'd be screwed if I turned myself in now. It's a conservative firm, Lenny. They don't make felony man-slaughterers partners."

90 "What about your car?"

91 "Slight dent," she says. "I can bash it into a tree, get rid of it."

92 "Talk to a lawyer."

93 "I don't want to tell anyone else about this."

94 "It's wrong."

95 "Legally, yes. I feel bad for the Laskos, but would knowing who did it and ruining my life really help them?"

96 "What if they offered a reward and I turned you in? Would that be wrong in Toni World?"

97 Is he messing with her? When she's desperate for his support? She rotates the heel of her hand into her eye socket. "Thirty pieces of silver? You're my *friend*. I've *trusted* you with this."

98 Lenny's quiet a moment. "Yeah, I'm messing with you." Another pause. "How are you going to live with yourself? At least talk to a lawyer and see what he says."

99 "You're sure taking the moral high ground, for a *drug dealer*."

100 A long pause. "Maybe so." More silence. "Look, I've gotta go. Think about it. Think about spending your life worrying that you've been busted every time the phone rings or someone comes to your door. It's not worth it. My two cents." He hangs up.

101 She goes over everything once again. It wasn't her fault. Why should she ruin her life over this stupid accident? She comes up with a plan to write an anonymous note and explain there was nothing she could do. She'll put a wad of cash in it, for Jody, to get therapy. Or clothes. Whatever she needs. It's Toni's fault that Jody found her brother like that, with half his head eaten away by coyotes.

102 Gordon. She can barely conjure an image of him.

103 Lenny. He'll get over it. Or not. If it had happened to him, if he had killed a child and fled—

104 It hits her then, the furtive kick underlying her dilemma, the cool thrill of getting away with all this, duping the dour detective. She presses her head between her hands and a memory intrudes, from junior high school. She'd been cruel to a boy—Jimmy Rodriguez—with a clubfoot and a little deformed arm that curled up to his chest with a useless, stiff-fingered hand that jutted from his wrist. She'd made fun of him, imitated his gimpy walk and arm, and called him a retard. Why? He had birth defects.

105 She wonders what happened to him, where he is today. She wonders if she could track him down somehow, find him, talk to him, and tell him how sorry she is. She wonders, if she begged him, could he forgive her?

106 She limps in circles now, in her living room, dragging her foot and folding her arm up against her chest in the Jimmy Rodriguez Clubfoot Shuffle. She sees her reflection in the polished black granite of her fireplace, and she wonders who in the world she might be.

Think about the Setting

1 • Where does the story take place? Think of the country, city, and some specific places.

____

____

____

2 • What details make this story appear very contemporary?

____

____

Think about the Plot

3 • In about six to eight sentences, summarize what happened. (Use the present tense in your summary.)

A woman is in a restaurant with her married lover.

4 • How did the following people contribute to Freddie Lasko's death? If you think someone is completely innocent, mention it.

Gordon: ______

Freddie's parents: ______

Freddie's sister: ______

Lenny: ______

Toni: ______

Think about the Characters

5 • What does Toni do for a living?

6 • How does Toni know Gordon? Where did they meet?

7 • What is Toni's economic or social class? Look for clues in the story.

8 • Who is Lenny?

9 • In Paragraph 17, the author says, "She didn't know why she had to toggle her self-destruct switch to feel alive." What does that suggest about Toni?

10 • Why does Toni decide to hide her crime? Think of at least three reasons.

____

____

____

____

Think about the Theme

11 • Consider why Alicia Gifford wrote this fictional story. What message is she trying to express? (There may be many possible messages.)

____

____

____

____

Vocabulary Boost (Pair Activity)

The following verbs appeared in the story "Toggling the Switch." Find a partner. Then, using context clues and a dictionary, determine what the words in your column mean. (The paragraph number is indicated in parentheses.) Be prepared to act out each word for your partner.

A		B	
stagger (12)	prop (18)	weave (23)	stroll (48)
sway (12)	nod off (22)	squat (27)	crush (50)
belt (14)	smack (23)	pound (27)	lean in (77)
doze (18)		tug (28)	

To develop your listening skills, visit the companion website.

Written Response

On a separate sheet of paper, write two paragraphs.

- In the first paragraph, explain how different characters are responsible for Freddie's death.
- In the second paragraph, describe the mistakes Toni made, and explain what she should have done or should not have done. Also explain what you would have done if you had been Toni.

Grammar

Should Have Done / Would Have Done

When you write the past forms of modals, remember to use *have* + the past participle.

She **should have taken** a taxi home.

Make sure that your conditional sentences are properly formed. Do not use *would* in the *if* clause.

had been
If I ~~would have been~~ Toni, I **would have taken** a taxi home.

Speaking •• Ethical Dilemmas

Find an ethical dilemma that is related to one of the following topics. For example, a family dilemma could be "Should parents split custody of children equally?" A medical dilemma could be "Should hyperactive children receive medication?" An educational dilemma could be "Should teachers pass students who plagiarize?" Then prepare an oral presentation.

business	education	family
medicine	personal	military

Structure

1 • Describe the dilemma. What is the problem? Describe a specific example that illustrates the dilemma.

2 • Describe some possible solutions to the dilemma. Present several different options. Explain what the long-term consequences might be.

3 • Link the dilemma to a real-life event. Have you, or has someone you know, ever faced a similar dilemma? Describe it.

4 • Make a final decision. How would you resolve the dilemma?

Presentation

- Speak for four to six minutes. You cannot read notes.
- You can bring cue cards with key words.
- Bring a poster that illustrates the dilemma. Your poster should be large enough for your classmates to easily see. (Do not plan to pass around pictures. It will distract listeners from your presentation.)
- Tell the story about the dilemma in either the past or the present tense. Be consistent and do not shift tenses.

C Visit the companion website for a list of ethical dilemmas.

Listening •• Judging When to Share Private Information

You will hear a discussion about an ethical dilemma. Randy Cohen, a *New York Times* ethicist, considers a listener's inquiry over whether or not to share someone's private information. Listen and take careful notes.

Listening Response

On a separate piece of paper, you will write two paragraphs about the dilemma.

1 • Summarize the situation. What happened? In your summary, include the following:
- What three dilemmas did Nick Lewis face?
- What two decisions must he make?

- What does Randy Cohen, the ethicist, suggest?
- What will Nick Lewis do?

2• Express your opinion about the dilemma. Include your answers to the following questions.

- What should Nick have done after he received his ex-boyfriend's email? Should Nick have behaved differently?
- In your opinion, what should Nick do with the information that he has uncovered?

Reading •• Compare Two Short Stories

Reading Strategy

Making Inferences

When the main idea of a text is not stated directly, you must infer what the writer means to say. *Infer* means to look for clues and then to make a logical deduction. For example, read the following paragraph. The writer does not state his opinion directly. Try to infer the writer's meaning.

> The band cost about $4,500 for the night. The hall rented for $800, and we figured we got a good deal. We had to decorate it ourselves. There were flowers on every table ($25 each bouquet), rented china and silverware ($1,850), tablecloths, tables and chairs ($900). The catered food worked out to be $40 per person, multiplied by three hundred. Well, you can imagine. This is not counting the dresses, the tuxedos, the photographer, or the rented limos. Sure, it was a "special night." It is too bad the guests of honour split up three months later.

Ask yourself the following questions.

1• What is the subject of this text? ______________________________

2• What is the writer's relationship to the guests of honour?

____

3• What is the writer's main point? ______________________________

Compare Two Stories

The next two short stories examine relationships from very different points of view. As you read each story, consider what the author is telling us about human relationships.

Reading 8.2

John Collier wrote science fiction. The following story is about a man's quest for an ideal relationship.

The Chaser

by John Collier

1 Alan Austen, as nervous as a kitten, went up certain dark and creaky stairs in the neighbourhood of Pell Street and peered about for a long time on the dim landing before he found the name he wanted written obscurely on one of the doors.

2 He pushed open this door, as he had been told to do, and found himself in a tiny room, which contained no furniture but a plain kitchen table, a rocking chair, and an ordinary chair. On one of the dirty buff-coloured walls were a couple of shelves, containing in all perhaps a dozen bottles and jars.

3 An old man sat in the rocking chair, reading a newspaper. Alan, without a word, handed him the card he had been given. "Sit down, Mr. Austen," said the old man very politely. "I am glad to make your acquaintance."

4 "Is it true," asked Alan, "that you have a certain mixture that has—er—quite extraordinary effects?"

5 "My dear sir," replied the old man, "my stock in trade is not very large—I don't deal in laxatives and teething mixtures—but such as it is, it is varied. I think nothing I sell has effects which could be precisely described as ordinary."

6 "Well, the fact is ..." began Alan.

7 "Here, for example," interrupted the old man, reaching for a bottle from the shelf. "Here is a liquid as colourless as water, almost tasteless, quite imperceptible in coffee, wine, or any other beverage. It is also quite imperceptible to any known method of autopsy."

8 "Do you mean it is a poison?" cried Alan, very much horrified.

9 "Call it a glove-cleaner if you like," said the old man indifferently. "Maybe it will clean gloves. I have never tried. One might call it a life-cleaner. Lives need cleaning sometimes."

10 "I want nothing of that sort," said Alan.

11 "Probably it is just as well," said the old man. "Do you know the price of this? For one teaspoonful, which is sufficient, I ask five thousand dollars. Never less. Not a penny less."

12 "I hope all your mixtures are not as expensive," said Alan apprehensively.

13 "Oh dear, no," said the old man. "It would be no good charging that sort of price for a love potion, for example. Young people who need a love potion very seldom have five thousand dollars. Otherwise they would not need a love potion."

14 "I am glad to hear that," said Alan.

15 "I look at it like this," said the old man. "Please a customer with one article, and he will come back when he needs another even if it is more costly. He will save up for it, if necessary."

16 "So," said Alan, "you really do sell love potions?"

17 "If I did not sell love potions," said the old man, reaching for another bottle, "I should not have mentioned the other matter to you. It is only when one is in a position to oblige that one can afford to be so confidential."

18 "And these potions," said Alan. "They are not just—just—er—"

19 "Oh, no," said the old man. "Their effects are permanent, and extend far beyond the mere casual impulse. But they include it. Oh, yes they include it. Bountifully, insistently. Everlastingly."

20 "Dear me!" said Alan, attempting a look of scientific detachment. "How very interesting!"

21 "But consider the spiritual side," said the old man.

22 "I do, indeed," said Alan.

23 "For indifference," said the old man, "they substitute devotion. For scorn, adoration. Give one tiny measure of this to the young lady—its flavour is imperceptible in orange juice, soup, or cocktails—and however gay and giddy she is, she will change altogether. She will want nothing but solitude and you."

24 "I can hardly believe it," said Alan. "She is so fond of parties."

Above the City (1914-1924), by Marc Chagall; watercolour and gouache; Christie's Images, London, England

25 "She will not like them any more," said the old man. "She will be afraid of the pretty girls you may meet."

26 "She will actually be jealous?" cried Alan in a rapture. "Of me?"

27 "Yes, she will want to be everything to you."

28 "She is, already. Only she doesn't care about it."

29 "She will, when she has taken this. She will care intensely. You will be her sole interest in life."

30 "Wonderful!" cried Alan.

31 "She will want to know all you do," said the old man. "All that has happened to you during the day. Every word of it. She will want to know what you are thinking about, why you smile suddenly, why you are looking sad."

32 "That is love!" cried Alan.

33 "Yes," said the old man. "How carefully she will look after you! She will never allow you to be tired, to sit in a **draft**, or to neglect your food. If you are an hour late, she will be terrified. She will think you have died, or that some **siren** has caught you."

34 "I can hardly imagine Diana like that!" cried Alan, overwhelmed with joy.

35 "You will not have to use your imagination," said the old man. "And, by the way, since there are always sirens, if by any chance you should, later on, slip a little, you need not worry. She will forgive you, in the end. She will be terribly hurt, of course, but she will forgive you—in the end."

36 "That will not happen," said Alan fervently.

37 "Of course not," said the old man. "But, if it did, you need not worry. She would never divorce you. Oh, no! And, of course, she will never give you the least, the very least, grounds for—uneasiness."

•• **draft** air that blows into a room

•• **siren** beautiful, tempting woman

38 "And how much," said Alan, "is this wonderful mixture?"

39 "It is not as **dear**," said the old man, "as the glove-cleaner, or life-cleaner, as I sometimes call it. No. That is five thousand dollars, never a penny less. One has to be older than you are to indulge in that sort of thing. One has to save up for it."

40 "But the love potion?" said Alan.

41 "Oh, that," said the old man, opening the drawer in the kitchen table, and taking out a tiny, rather dirty-looking phial. "That is just a dollar."

42 "I can't tell you how grateful I am," said Alan, watching him fill it.

43 "I like to oblige," said the old man. "Then customers come back, later in life, when they are better off and want more expensive things. Here you are. You will find it very effective."

44 "Thank you again," said Alan. "Good-bye."

45 "Au revoir," said the man.

•• **dear** expensive (British term)

Comprehension

1 • Is the old man's business legitimate? List some clues about the type of business he has.

____

____

2 • Although the text doesn't directly describe Alan, what can you infer about his personality? What type of person is he?

____

____

3 • What is Diana like? Look for clues in the text and describe Diana.

____

____

____

4 • What qualities will the love potion give Diana? Think of at least five qualities.

____

____

____

____

____

5 • Why is the old man selling the love potion for such a low price? Make a guess.

____

____

6 • What could a "life cleaner" be?

7 • What is the message of the text? (Note: the message is not directly stated. Try to infer what the author's message is.)

Reading 8.3

Kate Chopin wrote the following short story in 1894. As you read the story, consider the era that Chopin was writing in. Remember that this story was written at a time when marriage was not only considered a woman's rightful place, but a woman's only place. The story has been slightly abridged.

Kate Chopin

The Story of an Hour
by Kate Chopin

1 Knowing that Mrs. Mallard was afflicted with heart trouble, great care was taken to break to her as gently as possible the news of her husband's death.

2 It was her sister Josephine who told her, in broken sentences and veiled hints that revealed in half concealing. Her husband's friend Richards was there, too, near her. It was he who had been in the newspaper office when intelligence of the railroad disaster was received, with Brently Mallard's name leading the list of "killed." He had only taken the time to assure himself of its truth by a second telegram, and had hurried to prevent any less careful, less tender friend in bearing the sad message.

3 She did not hear the story as many women have heard the same, with a paralysed inability to accept its significance. She wept at once, with sudden, wild abandonment, in her sister's arms. When the storm of grief had spent itself she went away to her room alone. She would have no one follow her.

4 There stood, facing the open window, a comfortable, roomy armchair. Into this she sank, pressed down by a physical exhaustion that haunted her body and seemed to reach into her soul.

5 She could see in the open square before her house the tops of trees that were all aquiver with the new spring life. The delicious breath of rain was in the air. In the street below a peddler was **crying his wares**. The notes of a distant song, which someone was singing, reached her faintly, and countless sparrows were twittering in the eaves.

6 There were patches of blue sky showing here and there through the clouds that had met and piled one above the other in the west facing her window.

7 She sat with her head thrown back upon the cushion of the chair, quite motionless, except when a sob came up into her throat and shook her, as a child who has cried itself to sleep continues to sob in its dreams.

•• **crying his wares** trying to sell his products by shouting

8 She was young, with a fair, calm face, whose lines suggested repression and even a certain strength. But now there was a dull stare in her eyes, whose gaze was fixed away off yonder on one of those patches of blue sky. It was not a glance of reflection, but rather indicated a suspension of intelligent thought.

9 There was something coming to her and she was waiting for it, fearfully. What was it? She did not know; it was too subtle and elusive to name. But she felt it, creeping out of the sky, reaching toward her through the sounds, the scents, the colour that filled the air.

10 Now her bosom rose and fell tumultuously. She was beginning to recognize this thing that was approaching to possess her, and she was striving to beat it back with her will—as powerless as her two white slender hands would have been. When she abandoned herself, a little whispered word escaped her slightly parted lips. She said it over and over under her breath: "Free, free, free!" The vacant stare and the look of terror that had followed it went from her eyes. They stayed keen and bright. Her pulses beat fast, and the coursing blood warmed and relaxed every inch of her body.

11 She did not stop to ask if it were or were not a monstrous joy that held her. A clear and exalted perception enabled her to dismiss the suggestion as trivial. She knew that she would weep again when she saw the kind, tender hands folded in death: the face that had only looked with love upon her, fixed and grey and dead. But she saw beyond that bitter moment a long procession of years to come that would belong to her absolutely. And she opened and spread her arms out to them in welcome.

12 There would be no one to live for during those coming years; she would live for herself. There would be no powerful will bending hers in that blind persistence with which men and women believe they have a right to impose a private will upon a fellow-creature. A kind intention or a cruel intention made the act seem no less a crime as she looked upon it in that brief moment of illumination.

13 And yet she had loved him—sometimes. Often she had not. What did it matter! What could love, the unsolved mystery, count for in the face of this possession of self-assertion which she suddenly recognized as the strongest impulse of her being!

14 "Free! Body and soul free!" she kept whispering.

15 Josephine was kneeling before the closed door with her lips to the keyhole, imploring for admission. "Louise, open the door! I beg; open the door—you will make yourself ill. What are you doing, Louise? For heaven's sake open the door."

16 "Go away. I am not making myself ill." No; she was drinking in a very elixir of life through that open window.

17 Her imagination was running wild along those days ahead of her. Spring days, and summer days, and all sorts of days that would be her own. She breathed a quick prayer that life might be long. It was only yesterday she had thought with a shudder that life might be long.

18 She arose at length and opened the door to her sister's importunities. There was a feverish triumph in her eyes, and she carried herself unwittingly like a goddess of Victory. She clasped her sister's waist, and together they descended the stairs. Richards stood waiting for them at the bottom.

19 Someone was opening the front door with a latchkey. It was Brently Mallard who entered, a little travel-stained, composedly carrying his briefcase and umbrella. He had been far from the scene of the accident and did not even know there had been one. He stood amazed at Josephine's piercing cry and at Richards' quick motion to screen him from the view of his wife.

20 When the doctors came, they said she had died of heart disease—of the joy that kills.

Comprehension

1 • In Paragraph 1, we learn that Mrs. Mallard has heart trouble. What might be the real cause of her sickness?

____

2 • In Paragraph 2, her sister Josephine offers "veiled hints" about the accident. How does Mrs. Mallard's family view her?

____

____

3 • In Paragraph 3, we learn that Mrs. Mallard "wept with sudden, wild abandonment." What does this suggest about her character?

____

4 • In Paragraphs 4 to 10, Mrs. Mallard digests the news about her husband's death. What is her reaction?

____

____

____

5 • In Paragraphs 8 to 10, why does Mrs. Mallard try to hold back a strong wave of emotion that is gripping her? You will have to make an inference.

____

____

6 • The word "open" appears five times in the story. For example, in Paragraph 4, Mrs. Mallard stands "facing an open window." What does the repetition of the word "open" suggest about her situation?

____

____

____

7 • How did her husband treat Mrs. Mallard? Give specific examples from the text.

____

____

____

8 • How is the ending ironic? Did Mrs. Mallard really die of a heart-related illness?

____

____

To perfect your reading skills, visit the companion website.

Discussion

1 • Compare "The Chaser" and "The Story of an Hour." What does each story suggest about romantic love?

2 • How are the messages similar and different?

Speaking •• Comparing

Make a presentation in which you compare two works. You can do one of the following:

- Compare two readings that are in this book.
- Choose one reading from this book and compare it to another piece of art that has a similar theme. You can choose another story, a song lyric, a painting, a photograph, or a film.

  In an oral presentation of about four to six minutes, discuss how the two works develop a similar theme.

Writing Topics

Write a composition about one of the following topics. Remember to include a thesis statement and provide supporting examples. Before handing in your work, refer to the Writing Checklist on the inside back cover.

1 • "Toggling the Switch" presents a series of characters whose lives intersect. What does the story suggest about responsibility?

2 • In "Toggling the Switch," who is responsible for the boy's death? Describe the possible suspects, and then write a paragraph presenting your decision.

3 • Should social hosts be held legally responsible if a guest drinks and drives? Why or why not? Provide supporting examples from "Toggling the Switch."

4 • In your view, are penalties for drinking and driving or for committing a hit and run severe enough? You may need to do some research on the Internet to support your point of view.

To review some of the vocabulary studied in this chapter, visit the companion website.

5 • In "The Chaser," what is the author's message? How do the plot and the characters help to present the message?

6 • Write an essay comparing "The Chaser" and "The Story of an Hour." What message does each story have about relationships?

7 • What mistakes do people make in their personal relationships? Give examples or anecdotes from the readings in this chapter to support your point of view.

Writing Workshop

Essay Structure and Common Writing Patterns

1

Essay Structure

In the writing workshops, you will learn how to write effective essays. An essay is divided into three parts: an **introduction**, a **body**, and a **conclusion**. Look at the following example to see how different types of paragraphs form an essay.

The **introductory paragraph** engages the reader's interest and contains the thesis statement.

The **thesis statement** expresses the main point of the essay.

Introduction: ______________________________

____

____

Thesis statement: The public should pay more attention to real-life heroes.

Body paragraphs support the thesis statement. Each body paragraph focuses on one central idea. This idea is stated in the paragraph's **topic sentence**.
The paragraph is then developed with supporting facts and examples. Each supporting idea relates to the topic sentence (focus sentence) of the paragraph.

Topic sentence: Firefighters risk their lives to save others.

____

____

____

Topic sentence: Without police officers, there would be chaos in the streets. ______________________________

____

____

Topic sentence: Medical staff and researchers save lives.

____

____

____

The **concluding paragraph** re-emphasizes the main idea (thesis) and restates the main points of the essay. It brings the essay to a satisfactory close.

Concluding ideas: ______________________________

____

Writing Exercise 1

Look at the following essay. Using a highlighter, identify the following parts of the essay:

1 • Introduction: Highlight the thesis statement.

2 • Body: Highlight the topic sentences in three body paragraphs. Be careful because the topic sentence may not be the first sentence in the paragraph.

3 • Conclusion: Highlight words or phrases that restate some main arguments.

Alternative Culture

by Veena Thomas

In an era where alternative has become mainstream, what's an angst-ridden teenager to do? Dying hair punk colours has become passé. Goths with white face powder, dark lipstick, and lots of eyeliner no longer attract even a second glance. Everyone listens to "alternative" music. It has become increasingly hard for a teenager to rebel against the mainstream.

In other eras, youths had something to rebel about, but teenagers today have no focus for their frustration. The 1960s had the hippie era, as young adults rebelled by protesting against injustice, the Vietnam War, and the restrictions of society. LSD, marijuana, and free love reigned. Flash forward to the 1970s, when the punk movement came into existence with bands such as the Sex Pistols, and unemployed youths railed against consumerism. Kurt Cobain, in the early 1990s, became the rallying cry for a new generation of teenagers disillusioned with the confines of society. But what do those struggling to be different complain about now? Nobody is in the streets. Nobody is rising up.

Furthermore, what should a young punk wear? Previously, rebellious teenagers had to resort to shopping in thrift stores or making their own clothes to attain their desired fashion statement. Luckily (or unluckily) for them, society now makes it easy to dress like an "individual," and bizarre fashion statements have become acceptable. Companies make jeans that already have holes in them so young buyers do not have to wait around to get that punk look. If they want to look different, they can try Urban Outfitters, the trendy chain store for people fed up with trendy chain stores, where they can look "unique" just like everyone else who shops there.

With this watering-down of alternative culture, it has become harder and harder to shock anyone or gain any notorious press. Marilyn Manson, the press's former whipping boy and scapegoat for music as a cause of violence in society (witness the aftermath of the Columbine shootings), has faded from the public's view. Then Eminem became a strange symbol for the increasingly difficult quest to be different from everyone else and to shock society into paying attention. He got some press for his song about killing his wife, but today, nobody is paying attention.

Today's teens, with little to rebel against, find themselves wearing clothing that is mainstream and espousing ideas that shock no one. Perhaps to be truly alternative, people should not try too hard. Authentic is best, no matter what that might be. Teens can dress as punk or as preppy as they like and not let society's version of "alternative" control their actions. The truly cool can think for themselves.

Types of Writing Patterns

Narration / Description

A **narrative** composition tells a story and contains information about what happened. There are two main types of narrative writing. In **first-person narration**, you describe a personal experience using *I* or *we*. In **third-person narration**, you describe what happened to somebody else using *he*, *she*, or *they*.

Thesis Statements for Narrative Essays

The **thesis statement** controls the direction of the body paragraphs. To create a meaningful thesis statement for a narrative essay, you could ask yourself what you learned, how you changed, or how the event is important.

The accident made me re-evaluate my priorities.

When I moved out, I learned to be more organized and financially responsible.

Using Descriptive Language

When you narrate, you can include descriptive words and phrases. **Descriptive** writing often contains imagery that appeals to the five senses: sight, smell, hearing, taste, and touch. (See page 90 for detailed information about imagery.) Also, to make a story more vivid, you can use the following strategies:

- Use **adjectives and adverbs.** Adjectives give more information about nouns. Adverbs give information about verbs.

  Boring: She walked across the room.

  Vivid: The wiry, energetic woman walked quickly across the room.

- Use **specific verbs.** For example, *dashed* is more specific than *went*.

  Boring: He went to work in a hurry.

  Vivid: He dashed to his car and then sped along the highway.

- Add **details** to make the sentence more complete.

  Boring: The teacher looked at the bad student.

  Vivid: Mrs. Normandeau, a nasty teacher, snapped her ruler on the child's desk and glared at the young offender.

Writing Exercise 2

Write at least two synonyms for the words in bold.

EXAMPLE — That is **good** food. *tasty, delicious*

1• I **thought** about the problem all day. ______________

2• He is a **nice** person. ______________

3• She **hit** the strange man. ______________

4• The girl **laughed**. ______________

Writing Exercise 3

Rewrite one of the next sentences by adding information such as names and other details to make the image more vivid.

EXAMPLE — The baby cried. *Seven-month-old Amanda's piercing wails rang inside my skull.*

1 • The shy student spoke to his teacher.

____

____

2 • The boss was angry with the employee.

____

____

3 • The police officer arrested the young offender.

____

____

Narrative Essay Plan

Before writing your narrative essay, make an essay plan. Include specific details.

Sample Essay Plan

Introduction

Thesis statement: Travelling has taught me many things.

I: On my trip to Italy, I overcame my fear of travelling alone.
- **A.** People greeted me and wanted to talk when they saw I was alone.
- **B.** I met other travellers in the youth hostel.
- **C.** I played chess for hours with German and Spanish friends.

II: I learned to appreciate different foods.
- **A.** I realized the Italian food at home does not resemble the food in Italy.
- **B.** In Greece, I developed an appreciation for olive oil and garlic.
- **C.** I learned to savour fruit and cheese in France.

III: I realized that people are really the same everywhere.
- **A.** I met people who are generous, welcoming, affectionate.
- **B.** I also met people who were narrow-minded and intolerant.
- **C.** I discovered that everyone just wants a peaceful life, love, and a job that they can enjoy.

Conclusion: End with Tao saying: "The journey is the reward."

To read a student narrative essay, see "My Date with a Rock Star" in Chapter 2. Other narrative or descriptive essays are "The Longest Ride" in Chapter 1 and "The Living Goddess" in Chapter 7.

Compose It •• Write a Narrative Essay

Write a narrative essay about an event or decision that changed your life. Try to use some description in your story. Your essay should contain about five paragraphs. When you finish writing, circle five uninteresting verbs. Change them to more interesting verbs.

Comparison and Contrast

In comparison and contrast writing, you explain how people, places, things, or ideas are the same or different in order to prove a specific point. "To compare" means to look for similarities, and "to contrast" means to look for differences. You might compare two things to make judgments about them or to better understand them.

Thesis Statements for Comparison and Contrast Essays

The **thesis statement** controls the direction of the body paragraphs and shows what is being compared and contrasted. The first statement below compares youths from the 1920s with youths today. The second statement compares toys made for males with those made for females.

> Youths in the 1920s were similar to youths today.
>
> Toys reinforce gender stereotypes.

Comparison and Contrast Essay Plan

Before writing your comparison and contrast essay, make an essay plan. Include specific details.

Sample Essay Plan

Introduction

Thesis statement: As children become adults, their heroes change from fantasy figures to real people.

I: During childhood, most people idolize superheroes and action figures.
- **A.** They wear caps and superhero costumes.
- **B.** Batman, Superman, Wonder Woman, and Spiderman are popular.
- **C.** They want to have strength, learn to fly, and save the world.

II: During childhood, celebrities also become heroes.
- **A.** Children put posters on their walls.
- **B.** They dream about being a music star.
- **C.** They hope to be famous one day.

III: In adulthood, heroes become more realistic.
- **A.** Adults appreciate parents and family.
- **B.** They find role models at work and in college.
- **C.** Realistic dreams have realistic heroes.

Conclusion: Suggestion about finding a role model.

In Chapter 4, the essay "Put GI Barbie in the Bargain Bin" is an example of a comparison and contrast essay.

Compose It •• Write a Comparison and Contrast Essay

Write a comparison and contrast essay about one of the following topics, or write about the topic of your choice.

1 • two books, movies, or stories

2 • your generation and your parents' generation

3 • beliefs about college life and the reality of college life

4 • goals you had when you were a child and goals you have today

Definition

In definition writing, you define a term or concept. For example, you might define *culture* or *happiness*. In a definition essay, use facts, examples, and anecdotes to enhance your definition.

Thesis Statements for Definition Essays

In your **thesis statement,** indicate what you are defining and make a point about the topic.

Stalkers are not misguided romantics; they are dangerous predators.

A true traveller is someone who lives with the locals and learns about their lives.

Definition Essay Plan

Before writing your definition essay, make an essay plan.

Sample Essay Plan

Introduction
Thesis statement: Cults have certain consistent characteristics.

I: Generally, a cult is fronted by a charismatic leader.
- **A.** The leader doesn't accept other views.
- **B.** He or she expects loyalty and obedience.
- **C.** The leader claims to be enlightened or to have an elevated status.

II: Cult members are encouraged to break away from their families.
- **A.** They cannot be near people who might discourage them.
- **B.** Sometimes they consider their own family members as enemies.
- **C.** Case of Ron Girard, who left his wife in order to devote himself to his cult.

III: Cults take an emotional toll on members.
- **A.** They must act like the others in the group.
- **B.** Freethinking and dissent are discouraged.
- **C.** They become dependant on other cult members.

Conclusion: End with a prediction. As the fears about terrorism, global warming, and nuclear wars grow, so will membership in cults.

To read a definition essay, see Veena Thomas's "Alternative Culture" at the beginning of this Workshop. In Chapter 3, "Seeing Red over Myths" is another example of a definition essay.

Compose It ·· Write a Definition Essay

Write a definition essay about one of the next topics.

Culture **A celebrity** **Religion** **A good relationship**

Argument

Argument is the most common type of academic writing. For a complete chapter on the argument essay, see Writing Workshop 4.

Writing Workshop

Writing an Academic Essay

2

In most college courses, you will write academic essays. This chapter gives you some guidelines on preparing an essay.

Prepare to Write

There are various strategies that you can use to narrow and develop a topic. The most common strategies are **freewriting, brainstorming**, and **questioning**.

When you **freewrite**, you write without stopping for a limited period of time. You record whatever thoughts come into your mind without worrying about spelling, grammar, or punctuation.

EXAMPLE

What experiences have had an impact on me? I don't know. Maybe losing a job because I was late twice. It was embarrassing, but I'm always on time now at work. What else? The time I cracked my ribs when I rode my bike down a hillside at high speed. I wanted to be like those downhill mountain bikers. The problem was my bike wasn't very good, and I wasn't very skilled.

When you **brainstorm**, you create a list of ideas. If you need to, you can stop and think while you are creating your list. Once again, you don't worry about grammar or spelling—the point is to generate ideas. You can also make a list of **questions** to help you determine your topic.

EXAMPLE

Topic: War

- Why do nations continue to engage in war?
- When is war justified?
- Who suffers the most during a war?
- What is the best way to prevent wars?
- the impacts that war has on civilians
- following orders
- post-traumatic stress disorder

Compose It •• Generate Ideas

Use freewriting, brainstorming, or questioning to generate ideas about one of the following topics.

Travel **Heroes** **Advertising** **Mistakes**

Other topics: ____________________

Writing a Thesis Statement

A **thesis statement** expresses the main idea of the essay and is supported by the topic sentence of each body paragraph. Review the differences between a topic sentence and a thesis statement.

PARAGRAPH	ESSAY
A **topic sentence** states the main idea of a paragraph. It is the most general sentence, and it is supported by every other sentence in the paragraph. It usually appears close to the beginning of the paragraph.	A **thesis statement** expresses the main idea of the essay. It usually appears near the end of the introductory paragraph. Other paragraphs in the essay support the thesis statement, and each paragraph contains a topic sentence.

A good thesis statement focuses on a central idea. It presents the content of the essay, and it includes a **controlling idea** that expresses the writer's opinion, attitude, or feeling about the topic. The controlling idea can appear at the beginning or end of the thesis statement.

topic / controlling idea

Art courses should be compulsory in all high schools.

controlling idea / topic

School districts should stop funding **art courses**.

Writing Exercise 1

In your academic writing, you should include thesis statements in all types of essays. Look at the following example thesis statements. Circle the topic and underline the controlling idea in each statement. (To find the topic, ask yourself what the essay is essentially about.)

EXAMPLE — The intersection near this college is dangerous.

1 • Leaving the family home is an exciting and educational experience.

2 • There should not be racial profiling at borders.

3 • Three strategies can help you become a better public speaker.

4 • Alcohol advertising should be banned.

5 • There are several reasons for Australia's compulsory voting system.

Characteristics of an Effective Thesis Statement

When you develop your thesis statement, make sure it has the following qualities.

- **It expresses an attitude or point of view about the topic.**

  Your thesis statement should always reveal one complete thought. Rather than announcing the topic, it should make a point about the topic.

Announces:	I will write about war. (This sentence says nothing relevant about the topic. Do not use expressions such as *My topic is* or *I will write about.*)
Question:	Why do nations fight wars? (This question does not express a point of view about the topic.)
Thesis statement:	Greed, arrogance, and a desire for revenge fuel most wars.

- **It can be supported with several points.**

  If your thesis statement is too broad, your essay will lack a focus. If it is too narrow, you will not be able to support it. Your thesis statement should be clear enough to be supported with several body paragraphs.

Too broad:	Children are losing importance. (Which children are losing importance? For whom are they losing importance? This topic needs a more specific and narrow focus.)
Too narrow:	The average age of first-time mothers is approximately twenty-six years old. (It would be difficult to write an entire essay about this fact.)
Thesis statement:	Many couples are choosing to remain childless for several reasons.

- **It is a valid statement that interests the reader.**

  Do not make a vaguely worded statement or an obvious and uninteresting comment. Also, ensure that your thesis statement makes a valid point.

Vague:	Censorship is a big problem. (Censorship of what? For whom is it a big problem?)
Obvious:	The Internet is important. (So what? This idea is boring and obvious.)
Invalid:	The Internet controls our lives. (This statement is difficult to believe or prove.)
Thesis statement:	The Internet has a powerful impact on our personal, social, and working lives.

Guided Thesis Statement

Your teacher may want you to guide the reader through your main points. To do this, mention both your main and supporting ideas in your thesis statement. It is not necessary to prolong the introduction with extra sentences that provide details about your main points.

Weak:	Part-time jobs teach students many things. I will explain how they learn about responsibility. They also learn to organize their time, and they develop an appreciation for the importance of teamwork.
Better:	Part-time jobs teach students about responsibility, organization, and the importance of teamwork.

Writing Exercise 2

Examine each statement. If it is a good thesis statement, write *TS* on the line. If it is weak, identify the type of problem(s).

Q - question　　*A* - announces　　*V* - vague
B - broad　　*I* - invalid

EXAMPLE — This essay is about spousal abuse. ___*A*___

1• Why is the price of oil so high? ______

2• In this paper, I will discuss global warming. ______

3• Travel teaches people about tolerance, humility, and respect. ______

4• Some mistakes are very serious. ______

5• My subject is the torture of war prisoners. ______

6• Nursing is both physically and psychologically demanding. ______

7• Everybody believes in something. ______

8• Canadians are less patriotic. ______

Revising Your Thesis

When you plan your thesis, ask yourself if you can support it with at least three ideas. If not, you have to modify your thesis statement. Sometimes, just by adding a few words, a dead-end statement becomes a supportable thesis.

Poor thesis: Many students drop out of college.
(How could you develop this fact into an essay? It is a dead-end statement.)

Better thesis: Students drop out of college **for several reasons**.
OR Students drop out of college **due to emotional, financial, or health issues**.
(You could support this thesis with at least three ideas.)

Overview: Writing a Thesis Statement

To create a forceful thesis statement, you can try the following steps.

STEP 1

Find your topic. You can explore a topic to get ideas.

General topic: traditions

Brainstorming:

- Commercialization of holidays
- My family traditions
- Important ceremonies
- Why do we celebrate?
- Benefits of traditions
- Initiation ceremonies

STEP 2

Narrow your topic. Decide what point you want to make.

Narrowed topic: Initiation ceremonies

Point I want to make: Initiation ceremonies can help people make the transition from childhood to adulthood.

STEP 3

Develop a thesis statement that you can support with specific evidence. You may need to revise your statement several times.

Initial thesis statement: Initiation ceremonies serve a valuable function.

Revised thesis statement: Meaningful initiation ceremonies benefit individuals, families, and communities.

Compose It ·· Write Thesis Statements

Choose from the following topics or topics that your teacher has suggested, and write two thesis statements. First, narrow your topic. Then ensure that your statements present a point of view.

Travel **Heroes** **Advertising** **Mistakes**

EXAMPLE — Topic: *Mistakes* Narrowed topic: *Mistakes couples make*
Thesis statement: *When people first fall in love, they make several common mistakes.*

1 • Topic: ____________ Narrowed topic: ____________
Thesis statement: ____________
____

2 • Topic: ____________ Narrowed topic: ____________
Thesis statement: ____________
____

Generating Supporting Ideas

The next step in essay writing is to plan your supporting ideas. Support is not simply a restatement of the thesis. The body paragraphs must develop and prove the validity of the thesis statement.

Each body paragraph has a **topic sentence** that expresses the main idea of the paragraph. Like a thesis statement, a topic sentence must have a controlling idea. Details and examples support the topic sentence. In the following illustration, you can see how the ideas flow in an essay. Topic sentences support the thesis statement, and details bolster the topic sentences. Every idea in the essay is unified and helps to strengthen the essay's thesis.

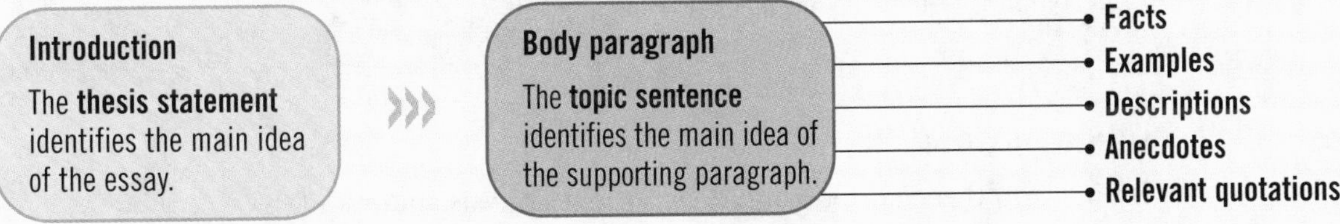

To generate supporting ideas, use the following process: First, brainstorm a list of ideas that back up your thesis statement. Then reread your supporting ideas and remove ideas that you do not want to develop in your essay. Also group together related ideas.

EXAMPLE

Initial Ideas

Draft **thesis statement**: Students drop out of college for many reasons.

Supporting ideas:

- skip too many classes
- can't adapt to college life
- feel confused about career goals
- don't have study skills
- can't afford tuition
- part-time job takes time away from school work
- financial problems
- lose a family member
- undergo emotional crisis such as a breakup
- ~~want to start their own businesses~~

Evaluate each set of linked ideas and summarize the connection between them. Develop topic sentences for each main point. Then list related ideas under each topic sentence.

EXAMPLE

Preliminary Plan

Thesis statement: Students drop out of college for many reasons.

Topic sentence: Some students face overwhelming financial burdens.

- can't afford tuition fees
- need to have part-time jobs, which distract from studying

Topic sentence: Furthermore, they may undergo an emotional crisis.

- lose a family member
- go through a breakup

Topic sentence: Many students are unable to adapt to college life.

- feel confused about career goals
- skip too many classes
- don't study or do assignments

Look Critically at Your Supporting Ideas

After you have made a list of supporting ideas, look at it carefully and ask yourself the following questions.

- **Which ideas could I develop into complete paragraphs?** Look for connections between supporting ideas. Group together ideas that have a common thread. Then create a topic sentence for each group of related ideas.
- **Does each idea support my thesis?** Choose ideas that directly support the thesis statement and drop any ideas that might go off topic.

Writing Exercise 3

Brainstorm three supporting ideas for each thesis statement.

EXAMPLE

When you buy a car, make an informed decision.

Ask family members what type of car they would prefer.

Research on the Internet about the specific models that you are interested in.

Keeping your budget in mind, compare new and used cars.

1 • First-year college students make some serious mistakes.

____

____

____

2 • There are several steps that people can take to help the environment.

____

____

____

3• When young people move away from home, they quickly learn the following lessons.

____

____

____

Writing Exercise 4

Read the following essay. After you have finished reading, do the following:

1• Create an effective thesis statement. The thesis statement sums up the point of the entire essay.

2• At the beginning of each body paragraph write a topic sentence. The topic sentence should sum up the main point of the paragraph in an interesting way.

Introduction

When I was a child, we had a daily routine. My parents both worked, but they got home about 5:00 p.m. They spent about half an hour unwinding over a cup of coffee. Then they worked together to cook the meal, and by 6:30 they called us children to dinner. We ate and talked together. The same thing cannot be said about many families today.

Thesis Statement: ____

____

Body paragraph 1

Topic sentence: ____

____

Overtime was not so common in the past, but today many employers expect their workers to spend an extra hour or two in the office getting the paperwork done, so workers don't get home until 7 or 8 p.m. Also, children's lives are more filled with activities. They might have dance practice, soccer, or music courses after school. When the adults and children arrive home at separate times, they make a sandwich or reheat leftovers. They do not sit down together to eat a healthy meal.

Body paragraph 2

Topic sentence: ____

____

According to the census bureau, a growing number of families have placed televisions in the kitchen. "It keeps the sofas and carpets much cleaner if everybody just watches TV in the kitchen," says Sylvie Labelle, a mother of four. Instead of sitting together, family members sit in separate rooms watching their favourite TV show or video. Daily communication, which used to occur at the dinner table, is disappearing and being replaced by a television set.

Body paragraph 3

Topic sentence: ____

____

Even a seven-year-old child can heat up his own dinner. Most parents don't want to cook from scratch after a long workday. Our grocery stores and specialty markets understand this need and provide families with a wide variety of frozen meals. Brigitte Lofgren says that the microwave oven is the most useful appliance in her house. "We all heat up our own meals. Nobody has to cook." When family members can easily heat up their own meals, it is less likely that they will bother to eat together.

Conclusion

Most families realize that the family dinner has disappeared. They assure themselves that because of hectic lifestyles, they have no choice but to stagger eating times. A television on the kitchen counter provides something to focus on during meals. And the quality of frozen meals is improving, so who really needs to cook? Yet it is tragic that the family meal, a simple and effective way to keep family members linked together, is no longer a priority in people's lives.

Write an Essay Plan

An **essay plan** or an **outline** is a visual map that shows the essay's main and supporting ideas. Read the next essay plan. Notice that each topic sentence provides evidence for the thesis statement. Supporting examples and details back up each topic sentence.

Sample Essay Plan

Thesis statement: Students drop out of college for several reasons.

I: Many students have financial problems.
- Support: The government cut financial aid to needy students.
  - Detail: Some students cannot afford books, tuition, or student housing.
- Support: Many have a part-time job to pay tuition and rent, but no time to study.
  - Detail: Describe Nick's schedule.
- Support: Transportation may be too expensive for student's budget.
  - Detail: The cost of a monthly train pass is high.

II: Some students undergo life-changing events and must leave college.
- Support: Pregnancy and childbirth overwhelm student's time and energy.
  - Detail: Anecdote about Ali, who was expecting a child.
- Support: A broken relationship can cause a student to feel emotionally fragile.
  - Detail: Three friends lost their focus after breakups.
- Support: A family tragedy can upset a student's college career.
  - Detail: Illness or death in the family can derail plans.

III: Some students cannot easily integrate into college life.
- Support: They cannot handle increased freedom in college.
  - Detail: Statistics about student absenteeism and lateness.
- Support: They have poor organization and study skills.
  - Detail: Example of Pat H. who forgot assignments and exam dates.

Concluding prediction: Increased student financial aid and counselling may help to reduce the dropout rate.

Writing Workshop

Enhancing Your Essay

3

Writing an Effective Introduction

Write your **introduction** after you have already planned the main points of your essay. A strong introduction will capture the reader's attention and make him or her want to read on. Introductions may have a lead-in, and they can be developed in several different ways.

The Lead-In

You can begin the introduction with an attention-grabbing opening sentence, or lead-in. There are three common types of lead-ins.

- a quotation
- a question
- a surprising or controversial statement

Introduction Styles

You can develop the introduction in several different ways. Experiment with any of the following introduction styles.

- Give **general background information**.
- Present **historical background information**.
- Tell an **interesting anecdote** or give a **vivid description**.
- Present a **contrasting position** or idea that is the opposite of the one you will develop.

EXAMPLE

Have good manners disappeared? In past centuries, a gentleman would spread his cloak over a muddy road so that his lady wouldn't dirty her feet. Twenty years ago, an elderly man or woman never had to stand in a bus because other passengers would offer up their seats. Times have certainly changed. Today, many people have a lack of consideration for others. **In contemporary society, parents and schools should teach their children basic good manners.**

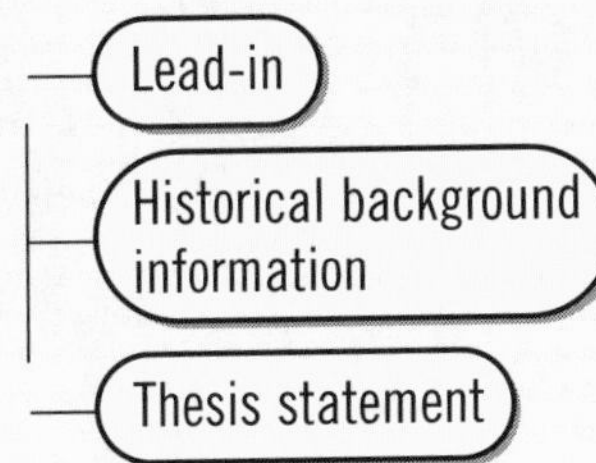

Thesis Statement Placement

Most introductions begin with sentences that introduce the topic and lead the reader to the main point of the essay. Generally, the thesis statement is the last sentence in the introduction.

Writing Exercise 1

Read the following introductions. Determine what introduction style was used, and underline the thesis statement.

1 • "A person who is not initiated is still a child," says Malidoma Somé. Somé is from the Dagara Tribe in West Africa, and he underwent a six-week initiation ceremony. Left alone in the bush with no food or clothing, he developed a profound appreciation of nature and of magic. When he returned to his village, everyone welcomed him and other initiates with food and dancing. Somé had passed from childhood into adulthood and was expected to assume adult responsibilities. The ceremony helped Somé and the other initiates feel like valued participants in village life. Our culture should have formal initiation ceremonies for adolescents.

a) Underline the thesis statement.

b) What type of lead-in was used?

☐ quotation ☐ question ☐ surprising statement

c) What is the introduction style? Indicate the best answer.

☐ anecdote ☐ general ☐ historical ☐ contrasting position

2 • Youths are dangerous. They join gangs, and they are responsible for a lot of the crime in our society. They drive too fast, they experiment with drugs, and they annoy others with their loud music. But is such a portrayal of youths really fair? In fact, most stereotypes about adolescents are incorrect and misleading.

a) Underline the thesis statement.

b) What type of lead-in was used?

☐ quotation ☐ question ☐ surprising statement

c) What is the introduction style? Indicate the best answer.

☐ anecdote ☐ general ☐ historical ☐ contrasting position

3 • Gang life, once associated with large urban centres in the United States, has become a common part of adolescent experience both in Canada and Mexico. In cities as varied as Vancouver, Montreal, Toronto, and Mexico City, youth gangs terrorize citizens. Many of the gang members have no strong role models at home, and their gang affiliation makes them feel like part of a powerful group. To combat problems such as youth gangs, adolescents need to be given more responsibilities in our society.

a) Underline the thesis statement.

b) What is the introduction style? Indicate the best answer.

☐ anecdote ☐ general ☐ historical ☐ contrasting position

4 • When does youth begin and end? In past centuries, the notion of "youth" did not really exist. Children went from childhood to adulthood with very little time in between. For example, in eighteenth-century Canada, most thirteen-year-olds worked in order to help support their large families. They would apprentice with older family members or friends, and they would develop skills that would serve them in their future jobs. Although opportunities for young girls were more limited, many rural Canadian girls did physical labour

on the farm, helped keep the family accounts, and contributed toward the maintenance of the family. In the 1800s, most girls were married by the time they reached eighteen. Today, we should shorten the length of compulsory schooling so that adolescents can take on more adult responsibilities.

a) Underline the thesis statement.

b) What type of lead-in was used?

☐ quotation ☐ question ☐ surprising statement

c) What is the introduction style? Indicate the best answer.

☐ anecdote ☐ general ☐ historical ☐ contrasting position

Writing Exercise 2

Write a thesis statement about one of the subjects listed below, or choose your own subject. Then write three introductions. Choose a different style (anecdote, general, historical, or contrasting position) for each introduction. Label each introduction with the style that you are using. You can use the same thesis statement in each introduction.

Beauty **Language** **Relationships** **War**

Using Transitional Expressions

To guide the reader from one idea to the next, use transitional expressions. The following expressions help the reader follow the logic of a text.

CHRONOLOGY (sequence of ideas)	SHOWING DIFFERENCES	ADDITIONAL ARGUMENT
• after that • finally • first,* second, third • first of all • in the first place • meanwhile • next • then	• although • even though • however • nevertheless • on the contrary • on the one hand • on the other hand • whereas	• additionally • also • as well as • in addition • furthermore • moreover

*Do not write "Firstly."

EXAMPLE	EMPHASIS	CONCLUDING IDEAS
• for example • for instance • indeed • namely • to illustrate	• above all • certainly • clearly • definitely • in fact • more importantly • surely • undoubtedly	• evidently • finally • in conclusion • in short • on the whole • therefore • thus • to conclude • to sum up

Writing Exercise 3

Write definitions or translations for the expressions listed below.

1 • although ______________________
2 • even though ______________________
3 • furthermore ______________________
4 • however ______________________
5 • meanwhile ______________________
6 • moreover ______________________
7 • nevertheless ______________________
8 • on the other hand ______________________
9 • therefore ______________________
10 • thus ______________________
11 • undoubtedly ______________________
12 • whereas ______________________

Writing an Effective Conclusion

Your concluding paragraph should do three things:

- It should restate the thesis.
- It should summarize your main points.
- It should make an interesting closing statement (a suggestion, a prediction, or a quotation).

Avoiding Conclusion Problems

To make an effective conclusion, avoid the following pitfalls:

- Do not contradict your main point or introduce new or irrelevant information.
- Do not apologize or back down from your main points.
- Do not end with a rhetorical question. (A rhetorical question is a question that won't be answered, for example, "When will people stop worrying about their appearance?")

Writing Exercise 4

Do the following:

- Highlight the topic sentence in each of the body paragraphs below.
- Write a thesis statement.
- Write a conclusion.

Thesis statement: ____

____

Body paragraph 1

First, many students and young adults stay in the family home because they cannot afford to move out. The cost of tuition has increased dramatically in recent years. For instance, universities in Calgary, Vancouver, and Toronto have all doubled their fees in the last ten years.

Additionally, the housing shortage and the rising cost of rentals make moving out a very costly option. For example, Leo Martin, a twenty-four-year-old student, still lives at home. He tried apartment living for one semester, but the stress of working thirty-five hours a week in order to pay living expenses proved overwhelming.

Body paragraph 2

Moreover, home is a comfortable place to be for many twenty-somethings. In 2005, *Time* magazine had a cover story called "They Just Won't Grow Up" about young adults who do not want to leave home. Why would they? Mom and dad pay for food, cable TV, and everything else. Laundry appears clean and folded on the bed. The fridge is always full, and warm meals are prepared and placed on the table. Leo Martin points out that it is his parents' fault for spoiling him: "I could never afford maid service. I honestly get treated too well at home. It makes me never want to leave!"

Conclusion: ______________________________

____

____

____

____

____

Making Complete Body Paragraphs

Body paragraphs are complete units. They have a topic sentence and supporting ideas. Each body paragraph must support the thesis statement. When you revise your body paragraphs, ensure that they have unity and adequate support.

Revise for Unity

A paragraph has unity when every idea in the paragraph supports the topic sentence. Check for the following common errors when you revise your body paragraphs.

- **Lack of unity**
  Some ideas in the paragraph do not relate to the topic sentence.
- **Rambling**
  The paragraph rambles on. It has several topics and lacks a clearly identifiable topic sentence.
- **Artificial break**
  The paragraph is divided into smaller paragraphs, and each smaller paragraph lacks a central focus.

Writing Exercise 5

Read the following body paragraphs and edit them. First, highlight four possible topic sentences. Then look critically at the paragraph structures.

- If a sentence or idea does not really belong, remove it.
- If the paragraph rambles on, suggest a paragraph break.
- If two paragraphs could be joined, indicate it.

Thesis statement: Television has a very harmful effect on people in our culture.

Body paragraph 1

First, televisions cause family communication to suffer. The TV is turned on from morning to night. Families install televisions in the kitchen, living room, and bedrooms. Thus, in locations where families traditionally congregated to talk, they now sit mutely—sometimes next to each other—staring at the screen. Instead of reading a bedtime story together, families deposit children in front of the television to watch a bedtime video. Also, people become boring when they watch too much TV. Their discussions revolve around television shows. People give each other advice by quoting Dr. Phil. When *Lost* was at its peak, my co-workers obsessively discussed each episode in detail. Many people consider their knowledge of TV theme songs as a badge of pride. Meaningless conversations about the television world are dull!

Body paragraph 2

Furthermore, the health of children has changed since the introduction of television. Before televisions existed, children played outdoors and spent most of their free time doing physical activities. Today, most children pass hours sitting or lying down as they stare at the television screen.

Body paragraph 3

Tyler Watkins, a ten-year-old from Regina, Saskatchewan, admits that he watches between six and eight hours of television each day. "I can watch whatever I want," he says proudly. But he is also overweight and suffers from asthma.

Body paragraph 4

Most sadly, many people have become addicted to television. My father, for example, has been a TV addict for many years. When I was a child, my dad turned the TV on as soon as he came in the door. We weren't supposed to bother him. Often, while the rest of us were eating supper in the kitchen, he would take his plate to the living room and watch the news. On weekends, he watched sports, and we would hear him yelling every time his team's players made a mistake. Growing up, we missed his conversation and company. When people are addicted to something, even if it doesn't seem dangerous, they should take action. They can always try to find other activities. Some food addicts, for instance, call each other and offer support.

Concluding suggestion: Try to spend a month without television.

Revise for Adequate Support

An essay has **adequate support** when there are enough details and examples to make it strong, convincing, and interesting. When you write your body paragraphs, do not offer vague generalizations, and do not simply repeat your ideas. Provide evidence for each topic sentence by inserting specific details. You might include examples, facts, statistics, anecdotes, or quotations.

Examples are people, places, things, or events that illustrate your point. To support the view that some local buildings are eyesores, the writer could give the following examples.

The car dealership on Labelle Boulevard is rundown.

The grey block apartment buildings that line Main Street are monotonous.

Facts are objective details that can be verified by others. **Statistics** are facts that are expressed in percentages. To support the view that transportation costs are too high for students, the following facts and statistic could be given as evidence.

> The monthly subway pass just increased to $260 for students.
>
> In a college survey of four hundred students, 70 percent expressed concern about the recent rate increases in public transportation.

Anecdotes are true experiences that you or someone else went through, and **quotations** are somebody's exact words. To support the view that lack of sleep can have dangerous consequences, the following anecdote and quotation could be included as evidence.

> When Allen Turner finished his night shift, he got into his car and headed home. On Forest Drive, he started to nod off. Luckily, a truck driver in another lane noticed that Turner's car was weaving. The driver honked his horn several times. Turner said, "My eyes snapped open and I saw a wall growing larger in front of me. I slammed on my breaks just before smashing into it."

Sample Body Paragraph

The following body paragraphs are excerpts from a larger essay. Read the paragraphs and notice how they are fleshed out with specific evidence.

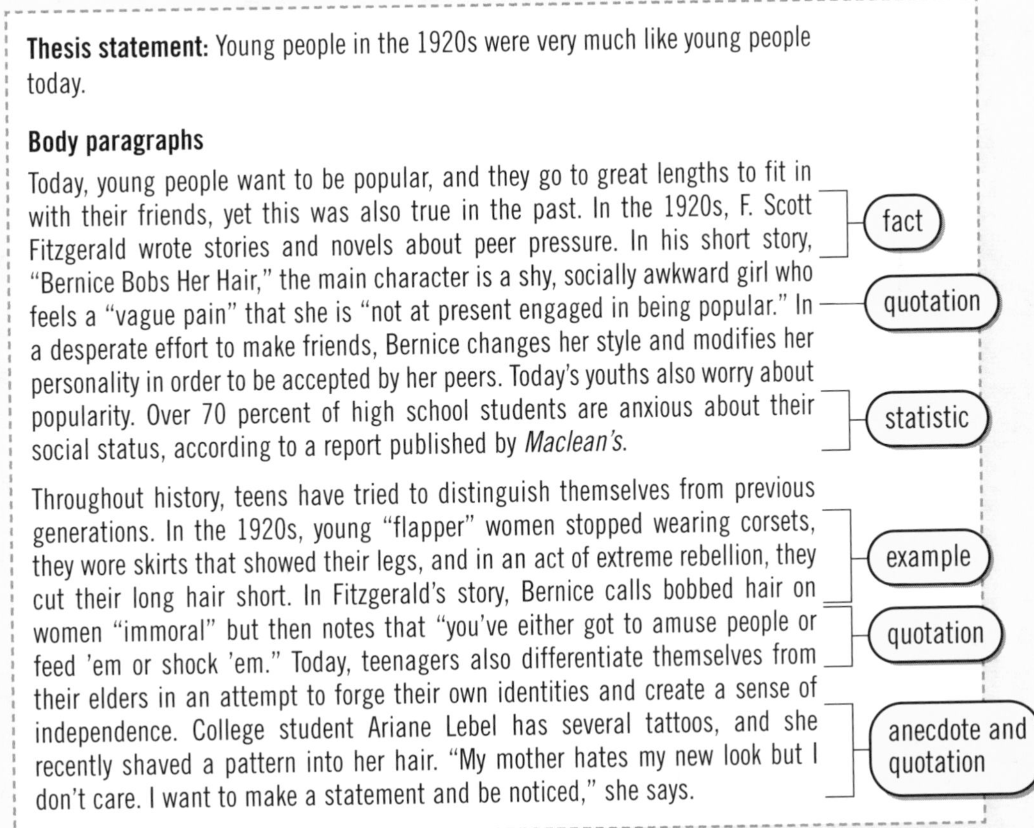

Thesis statement: Young people in the 1920s were very much like young people today.

Body paragraphs

Today, young people want to be popular, and they go to great lengths to fit in with their friends, yet this was also true in the past. In the 1920s, F. Scott Fitzgerald wrote stories and novels about peer pressure. In his short story, "Bernice Bobs Her Hair," the main character is a shy, socially awkward girl who feels a "vague pain" that she is "not at present engaged in being popular." In a desperate effort to make friends, Bernice changes her style and modifies her personality in order to be accepted by her peers. Today's youths also worry about popularity. Over 70 percent of high school students are anxious about their social status, according to a report published by *Maclean's*.

Throughout history, teens have tried to distinguish themselves from previous generations. In the 1920s, young "flapper" women stopped wearing corsets, they wore skirts that showed their legs, and in an act of extreme rebellion, they cut their long hair short. In Fitzgerald's story, Bernice calls bobbed hair on women "immoral" but then notes that "you've either got to amuse people or feed 'em or shock 'em." Today, teenagers also differentiate themselves from their elders in an attempt to forge their own identities and create a sense of independence. College student Ariane Lebel has several tattoos, and she recently shaved a pattern into her hair. "My mother hates my new look but I don't care. I want to make a statement and be noticed," she says.

Adding Research

One effective way to make your essay stronger is to include support from a book, magazine, or website. You can insert statistics, facts, or quotations from informed sources.

Essay without research

If you are not required to find outside sources to support your point, you can still make well-developed paragraphs. You can give anecdotes about your life, the lives of others, events in history, or events in the news.

Writing Exercise 6

Add details and very specific examples to make the next paragraph more complete and interesting.

Celebrities make poor role models. First of all, they simply entertain us, yet they are paid a lot more than people who do important jobs. ____________________

____

____

Also, many celebrities have bad habits, and they influence impressionable children. Some have problems with alcohol and drugs. ____________________

____

____

Finally, some celebrities modify their bodies to look eternally young. ____________________

____

____

Such celebrities make normal people feel inadequate. People should not idolize celebrities.

Writing Exercise 7

Make the next body paragraphs more complete by adding specific examples. You can include the following:

- anecdotes from your own life or from the lives of others
- quotations (for this exercise, you can make up punchy quotations)
- facts or statistics

Do not add general statements. Ensure that the details you add are very specific.

Thesis statement: Prospective pet owners should become informed before buying an animal.

Body paragraph 1

First of all, when families choose a dog, they should consider the possible dangers and the inconvenience. Some breeds of dogs can become extremely aggressive. ____________

Moreover, dog owners must accept that dogs require a lot of time and attention. ____________

Furthermore, it is very expensive to own a dog. ____________

Body paragraph 2

Some new pet owners decide to buy exotic pets. However, such pets come with very specific problems and concerns. First, exotic pets require very specific environments. ____________

Also, some exotic pets seem interesting when they are young, but they can become distinctly annoying or dangerous when they reach maturity. ____________

Avoid Using *You*

In some essays, the pronoun *you* is unavoidable. For instance, if you are telling the reader the steps to take to complete a process, it makes sense to use *you*. Look at the next example.

> After you have finished building the frame, cut the canvas to fit the frame. You should leave about two extra inches around the edge of the frame.

However, when you write about a general topic such as "Why People Believe in Spirits," or "The Causes of Wars," *you* is unnecessary. Look at the next example.

> Death is a frightening prospect. **Everyone** wants to feel like **he or she** will live forever. Religions provide **believers** with answers to the unanswerable questions.

Writing Exercise 8

Edit the next paragraph by removing *you*. Use a variety of replacement words.

The Internet has a large influence on students' and teachers' lives. Now, instead of going to a library, you can find material about any subject on the Internet. However, the Internet is filled with sites that you should not trust. Lobby groups put up sites that look legitimate. For example, pharmaceutical companies might have a website that appears to discuss attention deficit disorder, when the real intention of the site is to sell the drug Ritalin. New sites, such as Wikipedia, have gained a lot of respect, yet you must be careful because anybody can add information to the pages on that site. Your research can be flawed when you go to disreputable sites.

Compose It ·· Revise Your Essay

Choose a previous essay that you have written, and write a new introduction. Revise the body paragraphs to ensure that they have unity and adequate support.

Writing Workshop

Developing an Argument Essay

4

The ability to argue effectively is important in both your personal and professional life. When you debate which university to attend, which career to choose, or which movie to watch, you communicate your choice based on a logical analysis of the alternatives.

Taking a Position

In argument writing, you take a position on an issue and then defend it. In other words, you try to convince somebody that your point of view is the best one. The thesis statement of an argument essay should express a clear point of view.

topic — controlling idea

College students **should become more politically active.**

Your thesis statement should be a debatable statement. It should not be a fact or a statement of opinion.

Fact: Some car companies have produced electric cars.
(This is a fact. It cannot be debated.)

Opinion: I think that people should buy electric cars.
(This is a statement of opinion. Nobody can deny that you feel this way. Therefore, do not use phrases such as *In my opinion*, *I think*, or *I believe* in your thesis statement.)

Argument: The automobile industry should focus on the production of electric cars.
(This is a debatable statement.)

Writing Exercise 1

Evaluate the following statements. In each blank, write *F* if the statement is a fact, *O* if it is an opinion, or *A* if it is a debatable argument.

1• In our province, all car drivers must wear seatbelts. ________

2• I think that seatbelt laws are ridiculous. ________

3• Seatbelt laws should be abolished. ________

4• Many schools permit soft-drink companies to sell their products on campus. ________

5• I disagree with advertising on college campuses. ________

6 • College campuses should not promote brand-name products. ________

7 • In my opinion, abstract art makes no sense. ________

8 • A national art gallery spent millions of dollars on an abstract painting. ________

9 • The legal driving age should be raised. ________

Compose It •• Write Thesis Statements

Write thesis statements for the topics below or for topics suggested by your teacher. First, narrow the topic to make it more specific. Then make a debatable statement that clearly expresses your position. You can write three statements about the same topic, or you can choose different topics.

Spirituality **Memory** **Crime** **Relationships**

Other topics: ____

EXAMPLE — Topic: *Relationships* Narrowed topic: *gender roles*
Thesis statement: *People in committed relationships should share expenses and responsibilities.*

1 • Topic: ____________ Narrowed topic: ____________________
Thesis statement: ____
____

2 • Topic: ____________ Narrowed topic: ____________________
Thesis statement: ____
____

3 • Topic: ____________ Narrowed topic: ____________________
Thesis statement: ____
____

Developing Strong Supporting Ideas

In the body of your essay, give convincing supporting arguments. Find support for your views from reliable sources. You could use the following types of evidence:

- **Tell a true story**. Find stories from the news, or even include personal anecdotes to support your point of view.
- **Quote respected sources**. An expert's opinion can give added weight to your argument. For example, if you want to argue that the courts treat youths who commit crimes too harshly or leniently, then you might quote a judge who deals with juvenile criminals. If you want to argue that people are becoming complacent about AIDS, then you might quote a respected national health organization.

- **Show long-term consequences**. Every solution to a problem can carry long-term consequences with it. For example, in response to the terrorist attacks of September 11, 2001, many governments enacted anti-terrorism legislation. However, in some cases, the laws have been used to suppress legitimate dissent or free speech. The new laws could also be misused or misinterpreted by future governments.
- **Acknowledge opposing viewpoints**. If you acknowledge opposing arguments and then address them, you strengthen your position. For example, if you argue that school uniforms should be mandatory, you might address those who feel that students need freedom to express themselves. Try to refute some of the strongest arguments of the opposition.
- **Use emotional argument.** The strongest arguments can be emotional ones. Sometimes the most effective way to influence others is to appeal to their sense of justice, humanity, pride, and even guilt. However, do not rely only on emotional arguments! And do not mistake an appeal to emotion with an appeal to base instincts. If you use emotionally charged words such as *wimp* or *idiot*, or if you make broad generalizations about racial, ethnic, linguistic, or religious groups, you will seriously undermine your argument.

Writing Exercise 2

Read each of the following thesis statements and think of a supporting reason for each of them. Use the type of support suggested in parentheses.

1 • Children should not be spanked.
(emotional appeal) ______________________________
____

2 • The college dropout rate is too high in our province.
(logical consequence) ______________________________
____

3 • Pointy-toed stilettos should be banned.
(acknowledge an opposing viewpoint) ______________________________
____

4 • Fashion ads showing thin models are dangerous.
(anecdote) ______________________________
____

Compose It •• Generate Supporting Ideas

Choose one thesis statement from the previous Compose It section, and then generate supporting ideas and details.

Using "I" in Argument Essays

In argument essays, you should not use the first-person pronoun *I* in your thesis statement or topic sentences. However, it is perfectly acceptable to use *I* in an anecdotal introduction. It is also acceptable to use narrative excerpts when you provide supporting details.

Writing Exercise 3

Read the following student essay. Underline the thesis statement and the topic sentences. Circle any use of the pronoun *I*.

Introduction

"Why would I work for free?" my sister asked. I was trying to convince her to spend a few hours a week at the local senior-citizens centre. She refused, and she missed out on a valuable experience. Volunteer work should be mandatory in all high schools.

Body paragraph 1

Volunteer work provides students with valuable work skills and experience. Students learn to be punctual and reliable, and they develop social skills. Daniel Rowell works in a job placement agency, and he says that volunteer work can help students find that first paying job. When I volunteered in a "meals on wheels" program, I had to bring hot food to customers, and I knew that they depended on me. At first, I felt very shy around the much older staff and the customers, but I soon learned to feel at ease with people of very different ages and backgrounds. Later, when I applied for my first paying job, the volunteer work looked good on my c.v. Thus, volunteer work pays off in very practical ways.

Body paragraph 2

Moreover, volunteer work can help students feel like they matter. The act of giving time and energy to others is amazingly rewarding. Guidance counsellor Janet Cruthers says, "Students often feel isolated and lost. When they give to others, they find direction in their lives." In my volunteer job, I went into the apartments of housebound senior citizens, and I was usually greeted with a large smile. Most of the customers were so happy to see me that it made me feel happy too. The experience of doing volunteer work made me feel like I was actually giving back to the world and not just taking from it.

Conclusion

Our technological society isolates people, and volunteer work is a way to bring people together. The benefits are invaluable. Students across our province will benefit immensely if volunteer work is a part of the school curriculum.

Creating an Argument Essay Plan

Your argument essay plan should include a thesis statement that expresses a point of view, two or three topic sentences that support the thesis, and details that support each topic sentence.

Important

- Do not use *I* in your thesis statement or topic sentences. You can use *I* in an anecdotal introduction or in supporting details.
- Your topic sentences should support your thesis statement.
- Include details in your body paragraphs. If you did not do research, then include specific anecdotes from your life, from the lives of people you know, or from media events.

Compose It •• Create an Argument Essay Plan

On a separate paper, develop an essay plan for one of the following topics or a topic of your choice. Refer to ideas that you have developed throughout this workshop.

Spirituality **Memory** **Crime** **Relationships**

Other topics: ______________________________

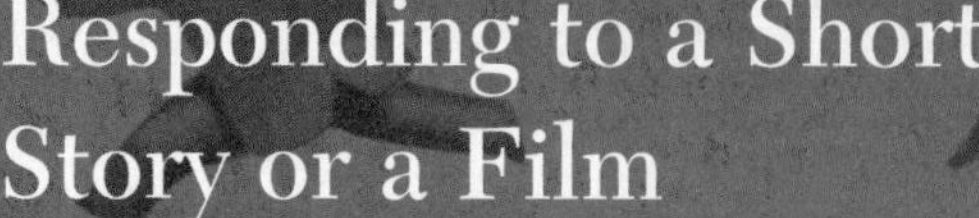

Writing Workshop

5 Responding to a Short Story or a Film

Every well-written short story, film, or novel has certain elements. It has a plot—or storyline—that engages the reader and makes him or her want to continue reading. It has a context, which is the time or places in which the action occurs. It has characters that the reader learns to appreciate and perhaps identify with. It has a message or theme that makes the story resonate with people from different places and eras.

When you read a short story or watch a film, consider the following elements.

Think about the Plot

When you discuss the plot, you describe what happens. Like essays, short stories generally have a certain structure.

- In the beginning of the story, we are introduced to the characters and the place of the action.
- A problem arises that makes the events more complicated.
- Generally the problem includes some type of conflict (a struggle between opposing forces).
- The conflict generates a series of events that build tension and suspense; it may end in a climactic scene.
- Some events happen to partially resolve the conflict. The central character may go through a transformation.
- The story concludes and the situation stabilizes.

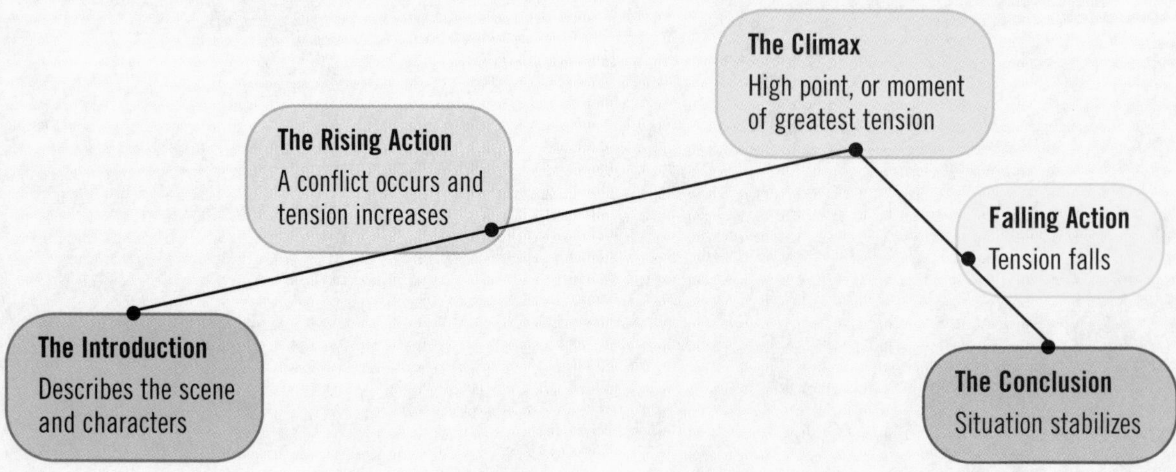

Writing about the Plot

When you summarize the plot of a story, it is important to boil down the story to its basic elements. If you summarize a movie or story plot, your entire summary should be about five sentences.

Compose It •• Write about the Plot

Choose a short story that you have read for this course. On a separate sheet of paper, make a diagram of the plot. Place the main events from the story on your diagram.

Think about the Setting

All stories have a basis in a particular time, place, and culture. The setting has an important influence on a story. When you read a short story, think about the time and place in which the story occurred. Also think about the social or historical context of the story. Ask yourself the following questions:

- Where does the story take place? Think about the specific location (house, office, park, and so on) as well as the more general location (suburb, inner city, town, country).
- When does the action occur? What was happening politically and socially at that time?
- What was going on culturally? Does the story address gender, class, or race issues?

Compose It •• Write about the Setting

Choose a short story that you have read for this course. Then describe the setting of that story.

____

____

____

____

Think about the Characters

Often the most memorable element of a short story is the characters. Although characters vary tremendously from story to story, they can be categorized into two types: those who evolve and those who remain static. Dynamic characters evolve during the course of a story. They may learn something new or behave in a different manner. Static characters do not evolve and their personalities do not change. When you think about character, ask yourself the following questions:

- What is the main character's background and personality?
- What are the main character's values, ambitions, hopes, and fears?
- Does the main character evolve or learn something new?

- Who or what is the main character in conflict with? The character can be in conflict with himself, with other characters, or with the forces of nature.
- Who are the secondary characters, and how important are they to the story?

Compose It ·· Write about the Characters

Choose a short story that you have read for this course. Then analyze the main characters.

____

____

____

____

____

____

Think about the Theme

Plot tells us what happens in a story. Character tells us about the people in a story. Theme tells us *the underlying meaning in a story*. The theme is a statement that provides insight into human existence. Themes are universal ideas.

Most authors do not tell you explicitly what their story means. Instead, the situations that occur and the reactions of the characters allow the reader to discover what the central meaning (or theme) of the story is.

Making a Statement of Theme

- **Theme must be expressed in the form of a complete statement.** For example, one of the subjects of "The Chaser" by John Collier is *possessive love*. However, that is not a statement of theme. To express this idea in a statement, you could write, "'The Chaser' illustrates the dangers of possessive love."
- **The statement of theme must express a universal truth.** Don't make narrow or overly generalized statements of theme. For example, someone suggested that the theme of "Conscience" is "People are all murderers." However, is this statement a universal truth? Remember that your statement of theme must be generally true.
- **Some stories may have more than one theme**. Several different statements of theme may be correct. One story may explain several universal truths. Most importantly, you must be able to support your statement of theme by referring to elements in the story.

Look at the following elements of the story before you make your statement of theme.

- After you have read the story, how does the title have a deeper significance?
- How do the central events illustrate a universal truth?
- How does the main character evolve? Does he or she develop a new understanding about life?
- Does one of the characters make a comment that might express the author's views?

Compose It •• Write about the Theme

Generate some statements of theme about a short story that you have read for this course.

____

____

____

____

____

____

Tip

Consider Symbols

Think about the symbols in a story. A symbol is a person, place, thing, or event that has an underlying meaning. For example, in "The Story of an Hour," the open window symbolizes Mrs. Mallard's desire for freedom and escape.

Create a Thesis

After you have thought about the story, the next step is to create a thesis. Develop a central idea for your essay. You can then develop your main idea by referring to the plot, character, setting, symbols, and theme. To create a thesis, you can do one of the following:

- Show that the plot, setting, characters, and/or symbols help illustrate the theme.
- Do a cultural analysis. What does the story tells us about gender, class, or race?
- Do a character analysis. What does the main character tell us about the human condition?
- Compare two stories and identify how they have a common message.
- Contrast two stories and identify how they look at an issue from different points of view.

Remember that your thesis must sum up the content and direction of the essay, and it should be expressed in one sentence.

Both "The Story of an Hour" and "The Chaser" demonstrate the darker sides of romantic love.

Compose It •• Write a Thesis

Generate a thesis statement for one or more stories that you have read. You can look for ideas in the previous writing exercises.

____

____

____

Use the Present Tense

When writing about a fictional story, use the present tense to describe the characters and their situations.

> In "Toggling the Switch," Toni **makes** an unwise decision. She **decides** to drive even though she is in no condition to do so.

When writing about historical events, use the past tense.

> In the 1990s, many governments **enacted** strict laws about drinking and driving.

Writing about Fiction

When you respond to a short story, remember the following points.

Do not write a long plot summary. It is boring for your reader if you explain everything that happened in a story. Instead, show something about the plot. For example, explain how it advances the theme. Keep your plot summary short!

Keep yourself out of the essay. Use third-person pronouns and not *I* or *you.* For instance, instead of saying "I think the main character changes," simply write "The main character changes."

Support your points with quotations. In your body paragraphs, include the exact words from the story that advance your main point.

Use the present tense to discuss the events in the story.

Punctuate the title* of the work correctly. If you are discussing a short story or essay, put quotation marks around the title, and capitalize the main words in the title. If you are discussing a longer work such as a film or novel, italicize or underline the title.

"Conscience" "The Chaser" The Lord of the Rings

*When you title your own essays, simply capitalize the major words.

Compose It •• Write an Analysis

Do one of the following activities.

1 • Write an essay about one of the short stories that you have read in this course. Develop a thesis, and then support your main point with evidence from the story.

2 • Write an analysis of a film that you have seen. Choose a classic film and describe the elements in that film.

3 • In his essay, "The Best Training for Life Is Fiction," Michael Korda asserts that the role of literature is to teach people about themselves and their humanity. By referring to at least two works that you have studied in this course, either support or refute this statement.

A list of classic films appears on the companion website.

Appendix

Oral Presentations

1

There are a few points to remember when you give an oral presentation.

Plan Your Presentation

- **Structure your presentation.** Include an appealing introduction. Use facts or examples to support your main points. Remember to conclude your presentation.
- **Practise.** Your teacher will not be impressed if you must frequently pause to think of something to say, or if you continually search through your notes. Practise and time yourself before your presentation date.
- **Don't memorize your presentation** or you'll sound too unnatural. It is better to speak to the audience and occasionally refer to your notes than to rattle off a memorized text.
- **Time yourself**. Ensure that your oral presentation respects the time limit your teacher has given you.
- **Use cue cards.** On cue cards, only write a limited number of key words and phrases. If you write your entire presentation on cue cards, you could end up getting confused and losing your place. Look at the example.

Text	Cue Card
The drop-out rate in the city is a major concern for government officials. At 40 percent, the rate is much too high. At the same time, those who drop out are experiencing depression and difficulty integrating into the workforce. Strategies to deal with the problem include smaller class sizes. Some experts suggest that the length of schooling be shortened so that students can graduate at an earlier age.	*40 % drop out* *depression* *no work* *strategies* *smaller classes* *earlier graduation*

Give Your Presentation

- Look at your audience members. Don't look only at the teacher!
- Don't read. However, you can use cue cards to guide yourself through the presentation.
- Use formal language. Don't say *stuff*, *it sucks*, etc.
- When the assignment requires it, bring in visual or audio supports. These can make your presentation more interesting.

Notes

